GOLFING

GOLFING

—— BY ——

J. R. HARTLEY

ILLUSTRATED BY
PATRICK BENSON

Hodder & Stoughton

ISBN 0 340 654 198

Set in Sabon by The Typesetting Bureau, Wimborne, Dorset
Printed and bound in Great Britain
by Mackays of Chatham plc

Hodder and Stoughton Ltd
A Division of Hodder Headline PLC
338 Euston Road
London NW1 3BH

Contents

	Acknowledgements	7
1	Teeing Up	9
2	Anyone for Ennis?	25
3	A Buggy for the Moor	39
4	Winning Ways	54
5	Miranda	69
6	The Caddie	82
7	Legal Eagle	95
8	They're Playing Our Shot	103
9	The McTeak	116

Acknowledgements

To Yellow Pages for the set up; to my publisher, Roderick Bloomfield, for the drive; to Patrick Benson for the draw; to Michael Russell for marking the card.

J.R.H.

I

Teeing Up

'The great thing about golf', said Tiger McCabe, 'is that the handicap really works. A good player can play with a less good player and have an exciting game. You know the story about Harry Vardon and the violinist?'

'Yes,' I said, because I'd heard Tiger tell it before.

Undeflected, he ran through it again. Vardon and a violinist played a match at St Andrews. The handicap took care of the huge discrepancy in their skills and Vardon won on the eighteenth. Someone asked him what would have happened if they'd been playing Brahms's violin concerto instead of St Andrews. He said he'd have lost ten and eight. No handicap could have saved him.

It was an untrue story that made a fair point. It was only a 9 iron short of a parable.

'I like that story,' Tiger said, 'it really sums it up.'

It should have done, but it didn't. He went on to say that if I had a 40 point lead in every game against the Wimbledon champion, I'd still be completely annihilated. You couldn't handicap tennis in the way you could handicap golf. I told him that if I had a 40 point lead in every game against the umpire's chair, I'd still be completely annihilated. But then I wouldn't be playing tennis. I hate it.

[9]

We were on our way back from a day out on the Wylye. Tiger had persuaded me to take him fly fishing. I guessed his approach would be over-physical and the fish would probably go into hiding for the rest of the season, but there was something so receptive about Tiger's enthusiasm that you felt you could always steer him in the right direction.

The Army, I'm sorry to say, had been less accommodating. He'd been 'rationalised'. It seems a betrayal when an institution that's so good at making you important suddenly informs you that you're not. Tiger hadn't got all that far, but he was on the escalator of commissioned rank and if there are two things that characterise an escalator, one is continuity and the other – assuming you've got on the right side – ascent. The last thing you expect is that it should stop. Tiger's had.

'It's ridiculous, isn't it,' Tiger said, 'all this cost-cutting?'

I nodded sympathetically, though I could see the principle wasn't in all circumstances absurd.

So now the McCabes were living in a Georgian rectory at the end of the village. The word was that Mrs Tiger had a reassuring bank balance that took most of the sting out of her husband's early retirement. Tiger spent a lot of time on the golf course telling people he was engaged on some scheme or other 'to earn a crust', as he put it, but I suspect the more substantial part of the loaf was already taken care of.

When we reached the river bank that morning, he asked what he should remember about fly fishing. Suspecting his weakness, or perhaps mistrusting his strength, I told him it was important not to press. You might make deeper indentations in the river, but you wouldn't catch too many trout. He said thanks, he'd remember that.

As we sat waiting for the morning rise I gave him some other tips I thought he might find useful. Then a fish rose, followed almost immediately by another; and in the excitement of the moment he apparently forgot everything

I'd said. He thrust his rod in the air and began to work up an excessive length of line, retreating from the bank as he did so. From quite far back in the field, he suddenly fired the line forward. The end of it landed in the river about forty yards downstream of the rise, but this didn't much matter because during his false casting one of several whipcracks from the line had snapped off his fly and about three feet of cast. So the projection of the remainder, wherever it landed, was no threat to the fish.

For the rest of the morning I had occasional success and he had none. He became explosively dejected.

'What am I doing wrong?' he asked me, as we sat by the bridge eating our lunch.

'You're pressing,' I said. Then, knowing he was a golfer, I told him to imagine he was just off the green, not beating into a headwind off the back tees. 'Guile,' I said. 'Delicacy.'

The images surprised him.

'You never told me you were a golfer,' he said. 'We must play.'

'I never told you I was a golfer,' I said, 'because I have a naive regard for the truth. I've exhausted the odd golf course, but I'm not exactly an habitué.'

'Come on,' he said, 'if you pitch and putt like you cast, you're halfway there.'

'I don't,' I said.

In fact I did – a bit. At Combermere, the boys' preparatory school in Dorset where I taught, I didn't admit to it because the bursar, with whom I had a somewhat competitive relationship, played a tolerable game – well, an intolerable game probably, but to a tolerable level of skill – and was longing to make mincemeat of me on the local course. He never stopped asking me when I was going to start playing and I always replied that my first love was fishing. It wasn't much of an answer, because there are months when you could be playing golf when you can't be fly fishing. Besides, the bursar was only too aware of my preoccupation with the rod: it particularly annoyed him that I was encouraged by the headmaster (himself a fly fisherman) to teach some of the older boys to cast; and, worse, that I would sometimes then get invited by the parents to join them on fishing holidays on water that was well beyond my means. I didn't let on to the bursar that on these holidays, when the weather was wrong, we occasionally went golfing.

So perhaps Tiger was nurturing a seed with his encouragement. Later that summer, fishing in strong water on the Dee, I missed my footing, hurt my hip and gave myself a nasty fright. My family, as well as my doctor, suggested that the time had come to curtail these more strenuous aquatics. It had occurred to me already, if only because both the salmon and the generous host were looking more and more like endangered species. I would still frequent the chalk streams, hosts willing, but for the Tweed and the Dee perhaps I could substitute Muirfield and Troon.

Courses like that, quite reasonably, aren't mad on complete rabbits; I'd have to show some degree of proficiency. I needed to know therefore whether this was achievable, so when I was staying with my daughter in the Midlands, I took a few surreptitious lessons. My short game impressed the professional, my long game, equally short, impressed him less. I was a little downcast. My daughter reminded me that if in the race between the hare and the tortoise I had to be the tortoise, I should remember who won.

'Slow and steady wins the race,' she added encouragingly.

I said I'd be happier backing quick and steady each way.

'You can't,' she said. 'Not enough runners.'

There was a course not far from where we lived in Dorset which I thought might suit my purposes. It was an easily manageable downland affair, with a long low clubhouse that had started life as a barn. I became a member and went to the professional for further lessons. He was a tiny man you could have hidden in your golf bag and taken round with you to get you out of bunkers; but he was a good teacher and under his instruction I was soon able to get myself an undistinguished handicap that I hoped would give me the bona fides to parade myself elsewhere.

Tiger meanwhile kept pestering me for a game. Finally I took the plunge and declared myself available for selection.

'Brilliant,' Tiger said. 'We'll play together against Eric and Deric. They like betting and we'll clean up.'

'You can do the cleaning up,' I said. 'I'll just concentrate on the golf.'

Tiger spoke of Eric and Deric as if they merely put the ass into assonance. It surprised me when he told me they sold cars. This is not normally the vocation of the gullible – in fact it's widely believed that the manufacture of car salesmen is part of the motor industry itself. Tiger explained that Eric and Deric weren't tailor made for the showroom; they'd come into cars after an unsuccessful venture into building. They'd set up premises as 'Eric 'n Deric Car Sales', with modest frontage on the street and a blackboard advertising their wares rather in the manner of a restaurant menu – even featuring 'Eric 'n Deric's Special Today', reduced to what seemed a giveaway price in relation to the car's appearance, though, as it usually transpired, less so in relation to its expectation of life, not to mention the purchaser's. The joint proprietors stood among the bargains, smartly dressed and wearing dark glasses against the glare of their personal jewellery. You could say quite a lot about them, but not that they weren't extravagantly congenial. They were always careful to make clear that their vehicles were sold with 'a spot of the old caveat emptor', but so engagingly that the emptor didn't always caveat enough.

They had prospered in surprising circumstances. One

night a competitor amended their sign 'Eric 'n Deric Car Sales' to read 'Eric 'n Deric Car Thefts'. It was a cheap calumny, but, as it turned out, a very expensive one indeed for the competitor. He had realised he might be suspected, but hardly expected to be caught. Unluckily, however, in completing his nocturnal editing of the sign with the help of a plank balanced between two stepladders, he fell off the plank and lay incapacitated on the pavement, his guilt evident for all to see. And though all's a fairly small number at three o'clock in the morning in the outskirts of Amesbury, there was an officer of the Wiltshire Constabulary to record the scene for the sleeping majority. Eric and Deric sued for defamation and other things besides. The judge came down firmly in their favour, awarding them damages and costs that finally resulted in their acquiring the competitor's business lock stock and carburettor. From that moment they began a period of steady expansion.

We'd play at Tidworth, Tiger said, four ball, best ball. He'd negotiate the bets and carry my stake if I preferred it that way. All I had to do was keep my game steady and pull out the magic wand around the greens. We'd aim for next Thursday.

'OK?' asked Tiger.

'I suppose so,' I said.

I drove up the A303 and turned off through Bulford on my way to Tidworth. I always like the ordered authority of Bulford Camp, with roads named after battles and generals of the First World War. I still half expect to see men in fore and aft caps painting stones white, and mounted adjutants trying to make their horses point the right way. But I think there must be awkward questions now about relevance and affordability. Still, as Tiger pointed out in a moment of un-expected philosophy, it's bad news for wars if you can't afford to fight them.

They cut trenches there in the First World War to instruct the soldiers for the Western Front – though whether they quite prepared them for what was coming is another matter. On the left, as you take the road to Tidworth, there are ranges and rather bullied open country. That morning a red flag was flying at the top of the hill on the right and there were lorries parked alongside the firing points, with parties of men standing about preparing for practice. In the middle distance you could see the lines of targets against their high protective concrete backdrops, with wings to field the ricochets. Further down the road there is warning of a tank crossing, where a long shallow incline leads up to the left to a track-torn area for manoeuvres, bordered with a line of trees and just the glimpse of the golf course running alongside. Thereafter the road turns in an extended S, the entrance to the course at the top bend, before you run on into Tidworth.

I was early. I sat in my car in the car park, with my bag of clubs leaning against the driver's door beside me. It wasn't a comprehensive array. There were two matching irons, a 2 and a 4, which I'd bought from the mini-professional, but otherwise, in deference to a mixture of realism and economy, they were distinctly *vieux jeu*.

My driver was the veteran of the party, protruding furthest from the bag. The head was inscribed with the name 'Leslie Rudd'. In my mind's eye I don't see Leslie in the group photograph of fame, but I'm sure he's up there somewhere at the back. My daughter suggested that he might only have been the man who put the Elastoplast round the loose cording at the bottom of the shaft; but I can't identify Leslie with anything makeshift. I see him as a minor professional who fitted up the likes of my father and his friends in their declining years, when they enjoyed hockeying round at weekends and thought themselves better players than they were. Leslie Rudd would have been my father's sort of man. Even about

Rudd would have been my father's sort of man. Even about the name there's a feel of good timing, and his wares were whippy, light and serviceable.

I'd only had one problem with the Leslie Rudd, and that was with the grip – after I'd been obliged to unwind it from the handle and use it as a tie. Four of us had played a round at a Scottish course during a fishing holiday and went into the clubhouse afterwards for tea. When we were about to sit down, the secretary told us politely that the club rules were effectively no tie, no tea, and that I, alone of the four of us, would not be permitted access to the scones. 'Perfectly all right,' I said without hesitation, 'I've a tie in the car. I'll go and get it.' And very shortly I returned wearing the Leslie Rudd grip and was adjudged, luckily by the merest of glances, to be conforming to the rules. As tea progressed, however, the leather strip started to ride dramatically up my shirt and re-form into curls, so that I had to crouch forward over the table, relieved not to be reported by the staff. Afterwards, when I reattached it to the handle, it never really settled, and eventually I had to have another grip put on. It seemed shabby repayment of a good turn, so I kept it in a drawer to make it think I'd use it sometimes as a tie.

I'd learnt to use the Leslie Rudd with caution. Too full a swing and you could be into a distressing slice. Time and again I found myself hanging to my left, thumping the club on the ground, helplessly begging the shot to straighten out. So I changed my technique on the tee, taking a frugal backswing and clipping my drive short and true.

I only had two wooden clubs – the Leslie Rudd and a light 4 wood, not signed by Leslie himself but very much his style. I had to adopt a slightly sunken stance to get the best results out of it; I think from its size it must have been a lady's club. For the big recovery shot out of a roughish lie, it was always the wrong choice and punished you if you thought otherwise, either by trying to break your wrists or by dislodging the ball a very short distance at an extraordinary angle. When I began to use it selectively, however, we became more of a partnership; and having achieved this rapport I was naturally loath to abandon the club for something more up to date. I shouldn't claim that either my apparatus or my outfit pinpointed me as a golfer of much status, but then I wasn't. My clubs were known as the Royal and Ancients. My appearance had more than a hint of Sherlock Holmes.

For my first professional encounter – I say professional because Tiger was proposing to venture considerable sums on the result – I was dressed, on instructions from Tiger, in a way that might encourage Eric and Deric to dismiss me as an eccentric and elderly tiro. I was wearing a pair of tweed trousers that I had bought in a job lot with an unframed watercolour at a Combermere Christmas sale. I don't remember in what proportions my £5 note had been allocated, but I had evidently overpaid. The watercolour, by the headmaster's mother, was a brown blodge that could equally have been a dachshund or a toffee, and the trousers must have belonged to someone with excessively long legs. They had to be hitched up in a roll around the waist as well as turned up briefly above the shoe. A strong leather belt, worn less around the waist than around the lower abdomen, maintained some sort of discipline over their general position. Apart from their undignified appearance, they were quite unusually prickly. I had to wear pyjama trousers underneath them; otherwise they turned you into a sort of vertical fakir.

Above the waist I kept up the competitive pressure with a frayed evening shirt and a metallic blue jersey that Miss Doberman, as we called the headmaster's secretary, had run up for me on her knitting machine. On the front, but not quite centre, it had a black and white goose with a very sharp bend in its neck. You'd have been ill advised to wear even Miss Doberman's best work, and this must have been easily her worst, though the model she favoured herself ran it close.

To top and tail the gooseberry, as it were, I wore a tweed cap with a front view like a failed face lift and cinnamon-coloured golf shoes with thick rubber soles that left an aggressive pattern on the floor.

Two Mercedes saloons turned up from the road and parked next to each other with that demonstrative *brio* I so dislike in motorists. The two drivers, Eric and Deric for sure, got out, stretched, adjusted themselves, and began conversing in loud salvoes across the roofs of their respective cars. I watched them through my offside window. They were both fortyish, rather flash, with figures just at that point when vanity finds itself in serious trouble. One jersey was canary-coloured, the other maroon. Their dark trousers had sharp creases, their shoes little tassels on the front. They looked like people you could order out of a catalogue. And before the seven days' trial was up you'd send them back.

When Tiger arrived a few minutes later, they'd already started their practice swings, checking at the top of the swing to make sure that the clubhead was square and their wrists were cocked correctly, then swooshing downwards to clip the ground and follow through. They broke off to greet Tiger with a chorus of laughter and whistles. As he pulled up beside them, one of them lobbed a dead blackbird through his open window with a cry of 'Catch' – which Tiger deftly did, then got out and playfully forced it down what he took to be one of their golf bags. He had driven the carcase to the very bottom of the bag and was beating it into a puree with the handle of the 5 iron, when it was brought to his attention that the owner of the bag was a retired officer who was packing up to go home.

I decided not to lend moral support in case my appearance raised further questions that the retired officer, already floundering, might find beyond his range. When a stranger runs up with a dead bird and starts using your mashie and your thoughts. So I stayed put while the clubs and the remains of the blackbird were shaken out of the bag and Eric and Deric wiped down the clubheads with the corner of the retired officer's car rug. Tiger then took the golf bag into the clubhouse and returned with it full of water, holding it upright while Deric stirred a golfing umbrella round in it. The retired officer stood by, contributing odd inter-rogatory phrases which never quite developed into sen-tences. In his position I think I should have been extremely testy. Nevertheless I could see that a degree of amicability had been restored when Tiger finally apologised again for the misunderstanding, wished him goodbye and led the others across to my car.

Eric and Deric looked momentarily taken aback at my outfit, but then, as we had intended, privately demoted me from the role of serious adversary. Visibly encouraged about their prospects for the match, they became ingratiatingly cordial. Eric infiltrated some conjoinerspeak about his uncle having been a schoolmaster too; he'd taught Latin, he said, in the North of England. Although this seemed unlikely, I replied approvingly that since the Roman destaffing of Hadrian's Wall the North needed all the Latin teachers it could get. At this Deric feigned considerable amusement, punching Eric in the chest to emphasise his appreciation of my reply. We went into the clubhouse in a spirit of camaraderie, and signed up for the round.

As we wheeled our trolleys across to the first tee, Tiger ran through the betting arrangements, which sounded both ad-venturous and complicated. Eric and Deric accepted every-thing without demur and we were off.

I was first to go. Out came the Leslie Rudd and the ball bounded away about 160 yards dead centre. I resheathed my club and stood back in some relief to watch the others. Tiger teed his ball up a little high I thought, although I didn't like to say anything, then put in some violent practice swings.

to say anything, then put in some violent practice swings. From his cries of 'No!', he must have felt he was doing something wrong. Still shaking his head, he stepped across to address the ball, wiggled and twitched, then slammed at it with a grimace of concentrated effort. There was an odd click and the ball soared upwards at a steep angle. We watched it hover and fall, bouncing in the middle of the fairway initially about sixty yards in front of us but spinning backwards to a fraction less than that. Tiger stamped in frustration, walked to the back of the tee and gave the club several more ferocious swings. Then he completely lost control of himself, hammered the driver on the ground, and shouted 'No' in a voice that must have been heard all over the course.

'No' isn't that indecorous, but it was a petulant – and for Tiger uncharacteristic – display. Four short ladies who were awaiting their turn behind the tee rebuked us with unspoken displeasure. Tiger had the good grace to apologise to them, but I'm afraid our cause was lost. They may have been lacking in vertical inches, but they were evidently skyscrapers of integrity and golfing etiquette.

Tiger nodded to our opponents that it was all right to go. Probably the incident had upset their concentration, because Eric hooked his drive and landed in some trouble far off to the left, while Deric finished on the other side of the thirteenth fairway that played back to the right of us towards the clubhouse. His shout of 'Fore!' should really have been given before the ball howled past a man who was shaping up for his second shot. From the ominous way he began walking in our direction I think he felt that too.

'What's he looking so fussed about?' Deric asked, setting off towards him. 'Hasn't he ever seen a sloppy shot?'

'Probably usually going away from him,' I suggested.

We watched them meet. The man stopped as Deric approached and put his hands on his hips. Deric walked straight past him.

I won the first. Then Tiger hit his tee shot dead to the edge of the hole at the short second, and things were going our way. When we started up the side of the course that runs alongside the edge of the training ground, Eric gave me my first experience of the golfing curiosity called a Mulligan. I'd heard Tiger agreeing with our opponents that we'd play 'Mulligans' for the first six holes – which seemed a rather generous running in period – but it was a new expression to me. It turned out to be virtually an amnesty for an out of bounds drive. I can't think why it should be named after an Irishman.

Eric hit his drive miles out of bounds to the left, in the path of a squadron of tanks which were labouring up the slope ahead of an anthill of infantry. Mulligan was invoked, and then he did it again – an almost identical stroke. At this he resigned his interest in the hole and, much to my dismay, clambered through the hedge to recover the two balls. There are procedures to anticipate most contingencies in the modern army, but dealing with a car salesman in search of his golf balls is still not covered. The tank commander called his machine to a standstill and asked Eric, very aggressively, what the hell he thought he was doing. Eric said he was hoping to pick up two hooked drives, if no one ran him over. The simplicity of his answer flummoxed the tank commander and the military action was temporarily suspended. Eric recovered both balls, and returned via the hedge with a wave of thanks to the men in khaki. I thought it showed exceedingly strong nerves.

The incident had slightly delayed us. The ladies' fourball had moved up to the tee behind us and they were making stately little preparatory swings. I waved back to them that we were on the move again, but I could imagine the disapprobation that was wafting towards us over this second breach of discipline.

Two holes later Tiger and I felt obliged to let them

'Fore!'

through. They had been joined by two younger women now, whom we dubbed the Fourballettes. They all moved steadily behind us like a permanent reproach. So when Eric and Deric had peeled off to the left to look for Eric's drive and were thrashing away in the rough some distance away, Tiger and I decided we must wave the ladies through. We hoped that Eric and Deric would see what was happening and mind their manners. The ladies sailed through with a sextet of thank yous.

As the round continued, Tiger and I maintained our upper hand. Not being at risk myself over the bets, I was happy to play a quiet supporting role; and with Eric and Deric getting more and more erratic and crosser and crosser with each other, I took my turn at twisting the knife. At the same time it became clear to me that the philosophy of my game must be to concentrate on the steady accumulation of respectable, unshowy scores. Eric and Deric were quite different creatures. What sustained them was the odd spectacular shot. Eric's 2 iron on the fifteenth would have done as much for him as the more careful husbandry of the scorecard did for me. I was a medal man, a tortoise not a hare, much more like the ladies who had been behind us and were now in front. It was all very well for Eric and Deric to laugh at their methodical little shots and say it was like playing tiddlywinks, but I'm sure that they had fewer sixes on their cards than Eric and Deric.

Tiger won a bundle. He congratulated me on my first professional outing. Eric and Deric pressed us for a replay, having quite recovered their good humour when Tiger accidentally reversed his car over the picnic the Fourballettes had just laid out. The ranges were silent, the tanks had gone home. For my part, what had been important about the day was that I had rationalised my game. The scorecard would be my gallery. I'd seen fishermen all my life who looked wonderfully stylish and cast a fizzing long line, but most of the time they were simply frightening fish that I'd have taken out. And so it must be with my golf – accuracy not distance. It wasn't very dramatic, but for my opponents it might be quite annoying.

2

Anyone for Ennis?

Since my golfing rejuvenation I haven't played in Ireland, but I promise myself a return to Lahinch – if only to remind myself of my wife's Uncle Reggie and Betty Grable's mother.

I should briefly explain about Uncle Reggie. He was charming, fanciful, wholly misdirected and a compendium of arcane information, much of which was probably untrue. He was a good fisherman, a keen sailor and one of the few motorists to have derailed a train. He lived in a largish house in Norfolk, which he rescued from decay at the expense of some ill-advised gentlefolk who parted with considerable sums and remained as paying guests. When his luck was running, he was more than generous, but keeping company with him was not without its hazards.

He took us once to Galway to fish Lough Corrib with the mayfly. It was a milestone in our holiday experience, and not just for the damage Uncle Reggie did to the hotel or for his investment in a stuffed bird to which he attributed mystical powers. So when two years later he suggested to Helen and myself that we should try the West again, we jumped at it. He had some fishing fixed up in County Clare. We'd be staying with a distant cousin of his called Ronnie McAlister, who'd finally retired from the Army to devote himself full time to indolence. He lived in a house called Ballydeckle, between Ennis and the coast, which was loved but untended in a way that the Anglo-Irish peculiarly understand. He had a wife called Mary, who was amiable but rather clumsy, one grown up daughter, Patsy, and a number of dogs that always beat you to the best chairs.

We flew to Shannon, where Uncle Reggie, in recovering his golf bag from the conveyor, raked two of our fellow passengers backwards onto his luggage trolley. They were fortunately quite elderly and unaggressive ladies, sisters I think, and no challenge to Uncle Reggie's conciliatory powers, which emerged in full flower. He insisted on putting their luggage onto his trolley and escorting them towards the taxi rank, but ran into a fire hydrant while addressing them over his shoulder about the probable fare. As a matter of policy Helen and I dissociated ourselves from Uncle Reggie in all theatres of travel and in any dealings with authority. This wasn't quite disloyalty. We knew he could be relied upon to get himself out of virtually any scrape without assistance, both because of his capacity for improvisation and because anyone in authority was usually extremely anxious to see him on his way.

The river was very low and we needed rain badly to rescue the fishing. So at breakfast on the third day, with the weather still holding, Ronnie proposed a round of golf at Lahinch.

'Yes, why not,' Uncle Reggie said.

'I didn't know you were a golfer, Reggie,' Mrs McAlister said, sitting with her elbow in the butter.

'You didn't know I played canasta with Henry Cotton,' said Uncle Reggie.

Mrs McAlister noticed her elbow was in the butter, removed it and began wiping her cardigan with the tablecloth. She evidently thought that Uncle Reggie could be trumped.

'Ronnie once played *golf* with Henry Cotton – at the Temple Golf Club.'

'Lots of people played golf with Henry Cotton,' Uncle Reggie replied, 'but you won't find many who played canasta.'

This was true. As true as that Uncle Reggie was most unlikely to have been one of them. As usual, however, his argument had a certain illogical force. He tended to knock people off balance. Mrs McAlister looked at her husband, who seemed reluctant to enter into the debate. Something told her, and not just family pride, that playing golf with Henry Cotton was more of a feather in the cap than playing canasta. She began to put this to Uncle Reggie, I thought persuasively, but rather lost the thread when he suddenly got up from the table and for some reason started doing gyratory stretching exercises, at the same time urging her to go on with what she was saying. Nobody could beat Uncle Reggie at the art of deflection.

It was no great distance to Lahinch – about twenty-five miles or so, on the coast. Ronnie, who was a goodish player, was a member there.

'Who's coming with us?' Uncle Reggie asked.

Helen and Mrs McAlister, not tempted, remembered they had some shopping to do in Ennis, but I said I'd go along for the walk and the sea air, and perhaps do some caddying for Uncle Reggie. In those days I'd played very little and I thought Ronnie would have quite enough on his plate coping with Uncle Reggie, without my holding up proceedings.

We took Uncle Reggie's hire car. Ronnie, thank goodness, was allowed to drive. Uncle Reggie sat in the front, treating us to a kaleidoscope of topics. Ronnie interposed occasional murmurs of surprise, just to show he was listening, while I sat silently in the back with Uncle Reggie's clubs, looking out of the window and wondering what it is about that country that so sets it apart. I think perhaps it's the serenity of scale, the way the landscape harmonises with the sweep of the ocean and the theatrical, precipitous cliffs of Moher. There's a placid strength about it all.

As we reached the golf course Uncle Reggie was still in full flood about bellringers' wages in seventeenth-century English cathedrals. His appetite for historical leftovers could make him seem more intellectually substantial than he was. I knew he was just an engaging charlatan, and so presumably did Ronnie, but he delivered his scraps and fabrications with such authority that people occasionally mistook him for a man of some academic breadth. This would have appealed to him. On the other hand, even Uncle Reggie wouldn't have expected to be impressing the two of us, which suggests that much of the outpouring was quite genuine enthusiasm.

As Ronnie and I hauled the clubs out of the car, I noticed Uncle Reggie's bag was marked with the name Harvey. It wasn't one of his usual aliases, so I asked him who it was.

'He was killed in an air crash,' Uncle Reggie said. 'I never met him. I just bought his bag from the professional at Brancaster.'

'Were they his clubs too?' I asked.

'No,' said Uncle Reggie, 'the irons came from a man called Harris – I swapped them for something that belonged to my sister – and I bought the woods at a sale of bankrupt stock in King's Lynn, fisherman's rib hats and all. Serve them right for playing golf when they should have been working.'

This was a fine criticism to be coming from Uncle Reggie. I refrained from comment, but Ronnie congratulated him on having a good eye for a bargain.

'Must keep on your toes,' Uncle Reggie said.

It's over a hundred years now since Tom Morris laid out the original course at Lahinch, reckoning it the finest natural course he'd ever played over. It was reconstructed in 1928 by Dr Alister Mackenzie, who was responsible for both Cypress Point and Augusta National in the United States. Augusta, familiar from hours of the televised US Masters, always looks like it just won a golf course competition at the Chelsea Flower Show. Of Cypress Point I know nothing except Bob Hope's joke about its exclusivity ('it had a membership drive and drove out forty members'). With marvellous natural advantages and the help of such pedigree designers, it's small wonder that Lahinch is the course it is. There were some modifications in the 1980s, principally to add length, but the club has a golfing formula that's hard to match. Sensibly, it sticks to it.

Uncle Reggie, apart from a tendency to overhit, was no slouch. He wasn't a great one for playing safe; he preferred the extravagant improvisation – which only occasionally came off. His approach play was his strong suit and he could on occasion be a formidable putter. I'm not sure he was actually a member of any of the Norfolk clubs, but he told Ronnie his handicap was thirteen and that wouldn't have been too far out. He talked a good deal to his opponents, which may or may not have been intended to put them off, and he was subject to rather dramatic moodswings; but things that might in other people have seemed just a little unsporting, in Uncle Reggie you excused.

The wind tends to come off the sea at Lahinch, but today it was only the lightest of breezes and the sun shone. So there were no superhuman calls on the players. For the first three holes there is a false sense of security – the first uphill from the clubhouse, then a par five back again. Next comes an attractive 150-yarder with a platform green. Uncle Reggie's tee shot hit the left-hand slope of the platform and bounded down and away. The lie wasn't that awkward, but perhaps the recovery shot looked harder than it was. Anyway, it seemed to demoralise Uncle Reggie and after two more shots he had retreated a further dozen yards or so, at which point he suddenly lost heart and conceded. We went to join Ronnie on the fourth tee, Uncle Reggie striding in front as I toiled behind with the heavy wicker picnic hamper balanced on his trolley.

Confronted with quite a stiff hill off the fourth and a good shot from Ronnie to follow, Uncle Reggie rose to the occasion and outdrove him. We enjoyed a brief period of effervescence, until Uncle Reggie's second lodged in a hidden bunker to the left of the fairway. He considered this for some obscure reason unfair and began to grumble about the construction of the course. Ronnie made it to the green, which is a generous size, parked his trolley at the edge and stood waiting, putter in hand, to see how Uncle Reggie was faring in the bunker.

There will be golfers who have seen a ball struck full toss into a bag of clubs parked on a trolley. I hadn't seen it before and I haven't seen it since; but of all the players in the world who could fluke such a shot and then claim the hole on the grounds of obstruction, I should always have kept Uncle Reggie as my first string. He alleged that he'd 'bagged' a shot before, though the previous time the ball had gone in first bounce. The player in front, who owned the bag, hadn't seen it happen and returned to his trolley after a shot from the rough to find Uncle Reggie upending his clubs onto the fairway in order to recover the ball. He didn't like that, and he didn't like the fact that Uncle Reggie had played before he and his friends were safely out of reach. Uncle Reggie responded to this by criticising the man for having no sense of occasion. This was a golfing freak. 'Speak for yourself,' the man said.

Ronnie, though sensing that Uncle Reggie was in volatile mood, adamantly rejected the claim of obstruction. He suggested that Uncle Reggie, if he felt strongly, should play the shot again from the bunker and he would move his trolley away from the landing zone. Uncle Reggie, who must have been rather surprised to have got out of the difficult bunker in the first place, elected not to accept Ronnie's compromise and played from where the trolley had been standing. The hole was finally halved, which was probably the least inflammatory result.

'This one's called the Klondike,' Ronnie told us on the fifth tee.

Uncle Reggie scowled up the valley in front of him and asked why it was walled off. I saw what he meant. There was a high dune, twenty-five foot or so, barring the path of the second shot. There was no way round. Uncle Reggie, touched by a spell of sustained inspiration, played the hole like a master. Then, at the 150-yard sixth, a mad, Irish, wonderful hole where you play over another monster sand dune to a blind green, he hit a sparkling 5 iron off the tee. Ronnie thought the line looked good, and so it proved. The ball lay scarcely a foot from the hole. A radiant Uncle Reggie tapped in the putt.

We'd planned to have lunch by the sea after the seventh, but Uncle Reggie thought this would be a propitious moment to anticipate events with a quick glass of champagne. I wasn't aware that we had any champagne with us, but Uncle Reggie stretched into his bag and produced from the bottom a bottle that Helen and I had brought as a present for Ronnie. It was warm and shaken up and not his property, but these were not the sort of considerations that weighed with Uncle Reggie when the celebratory mood came over him. He opened it, to a geyser of waste, and took a huge swig.

'W. C. Fields always kept a supply of stimulants in his golf bag in case he saw a snake,' he said, ' – which he also kept handy.'

I knew that one. Uncle Reggie always gave the old jokes a good run.

He wiped the top of the bottle with a cleanish handker-chief and invited Ronnie and myself to join him. There were glasses, he said, in the picnic hamper, if we were holding back for fear of disease. As it was Ronnie's bottle, much of it spilt down the front of Uncle Reggie's shirt, the sharing ges-ture wasn't out of place; but because our official stop was only one hole away and because I could feel from the weight of the hamper that there were other liquid goodies in the offing, I thought it wiser not to anticipate them. Ronnie felt the same. Uncle Reggie accepted our refusals and drank the rest of the champagne himself on the seventh tee, breaking off only to ask a goat what it was staring at. He then teed up and drove off with a huge cry of 'Down the hole', but the hole, as his ball soared away to the right, looked unlikely to be the seventh.

They have disappeared now but the wild Lahinch goats used to be a feature of the course. They would retire to the clubhouse when storms were on the way, and were regarded by the members as a sort of hirsute weather forecast. The day we were there, conditions were ideal and the goats were out in force. Some of them watched Uncle Reggie insist on holing out for nine, then came on to watch us start our picnic. We settled against a low dune and unpacked our wares while Uncle Reggie addressed us on the Armada.

Lunch proved an extended affair and before long Uncle Reggie fell asleep. Ronnie and I sat in the sand, feeling the touch of the breeze on our faces and listening in silence to the soft insistence of the sea.

After perhaps half an hour Uncle Reggie made a gurgling noise and stood up abruptly.

'Why don't you take over?' he said to me. Then he turned and walked off unsteadily in the direction of the clubhouse. Ronnie, sitting hands on knees, turned to me and raised his eyebrows for my reply.

'Can you stand it?' I asked.

'We'll take it slowly,' Ronnie said.

I went to pick up Uncle Reggie's bag. The goats dispersed around it. The strap and the fisherman's rib hats had disappeared. The cause of the Lahinch goats' demise has never been satisfactorily explained, but it's supposed that they ate something poisonous. Their gluttony that lunchtime could explain it.

Poor patient Ronnie. I was a very occasional golfer in those days, and the combination of lunch, inexperience and the challenge of the course didn't make this one of the better occasions. I still had the picnic hamper balanced on the trolley as we shoehorned ourselves back into play. The par for those eleven holes is forty-four; I completed them rather in excess of that. I couldn't be entirely precise, because after hitting two balls into the water at the twelfth, where your drive has to carry 150 yards to dry land, we decided I'd better move on to safety before I disposed of all the ammunition. And if I say that all the while my short game and my putting were really not too bad, it gives you some idea of the frustrations of the rest.

Ronnie kept on giving me tips. After my fluffed shot on the fourteenth, he suggested I was standing too close to the ball. I was only too aware of this. Until I actually struck the ball any appreciable distance, I didn't see how the situation was going to improve.

'No,' he said, 'your swing's too steep.'

He was right. It wasn't just Uncle Reggie's clubs, although there was no knowing what mysterious forces might be at work there. I tried giving myself a bit more room – at first too much, but then, manoeuvred into place by Ronnie, I started to clip the ball off the tee. The trouble was that on the back nine at Lahinch you need to be doing a little more than that. Aside from the twelfth, with the carry over the water which I failed to beat, the sixteenth, the last short hole, is all carry, with no fairway at all between tee and green. It's only 179 yards, but that's not much consolation if your best shot's 150. It's a frustrating piece of arithmetic.

I came shamefacedly up the eighteenth, feeling there were contemptuous eyes watching from the clubhouse and possibly nervous ones on the fifth and sixth, which you have to cross. But perhaps I was being over-defensive. The Irish attitude to a shambles, if only for reasons of familiarity, is quite relaxed; and I had the shelter of Ronnie's evident popularity at the club. As it was, Providence smiled on me as I closed in on the green, and I rolled one in from twenty feet. The club secretary, who had come down to watch, applauded generously, though perhaps only in relief that I'd finished the round.

I returned the trolley and followed Ronnie into the clubhouse, carrying the picnic hamper in my left hand with Uncle Reggie's strapless bag balanced under my right arm. I wasn't looking forward to breaking the news to him that the goats had eaten both his strap and the fisherman's rib hats. I knew it was the sort of thing that would considerably affront him.

I'd expected to see him asleep in a chair or regaling some trapped member with useless information, but there was no sign of him. Ronnie and I tidied ourselves up. When we came back to the bar, a very genial Irishman came across to say that Colonel Harvey had gone on.

Uncle Reggie's assumed identity was no novelty. He was known to favour a military persona, particularly in countries with a turbulent history. And his choice of surname was at least consistent with the name on his golf bag, even if with nothing else in his possession.

'Gone on?' I said. 'Did he say where?'

Our friend said he'd left with Bender Burke. He was going to show Bender the house where Betty Grable's mother once lived. It had to be said that the Colonel, in fact both of them, seemed a little under the weather.

I didn't know much about Betty Grable's parentage, but had I been a betting man I should have been looking for her mother's house not less than three thousand miles from Lahinch. West rather than east. Lighting on it so conveniently close to Ballydeckle smacked very much of Uncle Reggie in need of a lift.

'The Colonel's knowledgeable about the ladies of stage and screen,' I told our friend.

'It's a new one on me,' he said. 'I'd never heard that the lady was from these parts.'

'No,' I agreed, 'I don't think I had.'

The big surprise was that Uncle Reggie had left us the car. The small surprise was that he hadn't left us the keys. Our friend shrugged this off as a minor inconvenience and said he'd 'wire it' for us. We said that was very kind but there was an additional problem. All the doors were locked. It was a hire car and force probably wasn't an option.

'As you wish,' said our friend, 'but it's no trouble.'

We thanked him for his offer but decided instead to telephone Ballydeckle. Mrs McAlister answered.

'Where are you?' she asked.

'At Lahinch,' I said. 'There's a shortage of car keys. Is Uncle Reggie there?'

'No,' said Mrs McAlister, 'he's gone out again. But he left me the keys. Have a word with Helen.'

My wife appeared in Ronnie's car about three-quarters of an hour later. 'What's going on?' she asked. 'Uncle Reggie arrived with a frightful man called Bender. Something to do with Betty Grable.'

'Betty Grable's mother,' I corrected her.

'That's something to do with Betty Grable, isn't it?'

'Yes,' I agreed, 'Betty Grable's mother is quite a lot to do with Betty Grable, but Bender was misled by your Uncle

Reggie into thinking that Betty Grable's mother lived, before she became Betty Grable's mother, somewhere very close to Ballydeckle, if not Ballydeckle itself.'

'And did she?'

'I don't think that would be a factor in your Uncle Reggie's calculations. I'm not saying categorically that she didn't, but from what I know of Uncle Reggie I think it's at best unlikely. I suspect she was simply a ruse to get Uncle Reggie a lift home.'

We loaded the clubs into the hire car. Ronnie set off in his car and we followed behind. After a couple of miles Helen suddenly asked whether Betty Grable was 'the one with the legs'.

Yes, I said, Betty Grable was well known in that connection. And that, until we got back to Ballydeckle, was the end of it.

There was no sign of Uncle Reggie when we came into the drawing room. Mrs McAlister was sitting in an armchair eating a slice of chocolate cake, apparently unaware that one of the dogs was standing on the table behind her eating the rest.

'What have you done with Uncle Reggie?' I asked.

She said he'd gone into Ennis with Bender Burke. They were on the history trail.

It surprised me that Bender was still in the market for historical detail, and surprised me even more that Uncle Reggie, having cadged his lift home, was still in the market for Bender.

Mrs McAlister agreed with that. She said Bender had been somewhat short-changed by Uncle Reggie over his visit to the house. He and Uncle Reggie had arrived at Ballydeckle in high spirits. Mrs McAlister knew Bender by sight (and it wasn't one she much liked), having met him once or twice at Lahinch. Putting two and two together, a precarious sum when dealing with Uncle Reggie's *modus operandi*, she guessed that Uncle Reggie must be using Bender, since there could be no reason – even if you were obviously inebriated, as Uncle Reggie was – for any disinterested social relations.

Even so, she was taken aback when Uncle Reggie asked her if he could show Bender the Turret Room where Betty Grable's mother had been born. She said 'Yes, of course', but the look of bafflement on her face probably wasn't the collusion for which Uncle Reggie had been hoping. She warned them that the room wasn't very tidy.

In fact it wasn't very untidy either, since the only contents of the room – which the McAlisters considered too damp, small and unpleasant to use – were a Victorian washstand, a huge portrait oil of no quality with a hole the size of a plate in the middle, and a small seized up lawn mower. It was hardly a shrine.

When Bender came downstairs again with Uncle Reggie, he seemed less than thunderstruck. Nothing about Mrs McAlister's reaction seemed to endorse Uncle Reggie's claims about the actress's mother. Uncle Reggie, sensing things weren't going all that well, said he hoped he hadn't brought him on a wild goose chase – he had the feeling that Bender was expecting something more obviously commemorative. No, said Bender, not at all, and he'd been very interested in everything that Uncle Reggie had been telling him in the car.

'What was he telling you in the car?' Mrs McAlister asked, noticing that Uncle Reggie was indicating behind Bender's back that every effort should be made to get rid of the man.

'Historical stuff,' Bender said.

Mrs McAlister then mischievously suggested that Bender should go into Ennis with Uncle Reggie and show him the historical sights. Bender warmed to this suggestion. Uncle Reggie, who could only shake his head in disbelief at his hostess's betrayal of him, was ushered out again to the car and driven off to Ennis.

So we were all present to see Uncle Reggie's chastened return. He came into the drawing room first and merely raised his eyes to the ceiling in an expression of exhaustion and despair. Bender, by contrast, seemed well satisfied and told us that the two of them had really squeezed Ennis's historical lemon.

I then made the mistake of questioning how substantial a lemon that might be, which drew a lengthy response from Bender that all of us could have done without. We sank into our chairs, trying to maintain expressions of interest on our frozen faces.

We finally disposed of Bender when it was almost time for dinner. Ronnie resolutely refused to ask him to stay, but he played it down to the wire. Uncle Reggie was by this time stretched out on the sofa with two dogs on top of him, drained of all historical anecdote. I'd never seen him so deflated. Mrs McAlister had pulled off an excellent reprisal.

'Lord have mercy,' Uncle Reggie said, as through the un-curtained drawing room windows we saw Bender's head-lights finally ranging away down the drive.

'Not today, I'm afraid,' I told him. 'The goats ate the strap of your golf bag.'

He stared at me blankly.

'The goats?'

'The goats,' I repeated.

'The bastards,' said Uncle Reggie, 'I knew they had it in for me. I've a good mind to shoot one of them and have it made into a new bag.'

'Choose the right one,' I said, 'and you'll get a strap for free.'

3
A Buggy for the Moor

Gervase Marston was known almost universally as 'The Moor'. This was because he was called Marston and had a swarthy appearance, though the full implications of the joke may have eluded some of his acquaintances in clubland, who tended to be stronger on racial characteristics than the battles of the English Civil War. He had sidestepped any pretence of work by marrying a couple of rich women. The first of them, whose looks ran a poor second to her resources, had a fortune that derived from acetylene lamps. She finally dismissed him for repeated infidelity, only to see him almost immediately taken on – to her chagrin – by someone even richer and, if possible, plainer. It's a common phenomenon that men and women take on new partners who are marginally adapted versions of their predecessors; which is why, or so it was said, the Moor's second wife looked so like an acetylene lamp.

I didn't myself have a chance of making comparisons, because the first marriage was long past when I met the Moor up on the Dee, and the second wife didn't like fishing and never appeared at the lodge, although she rang up every evening to ask how he'd got on. She was clearly very proud of him; I was told she even dredged up exploits from his amatory past to prove she had landed a Lothario, but the more worldly-wise suspected that his ardour was directed more towards her portfolio than her unprovocative body. Still, you never know. Very funny things happen in bedrooms, and she was a good woman who deserved romance.

The Moor and I had little in common except a penchant for fishing and a generous host who asked us both up to his lodge. But we struck up a serviceable friendship. I suppose what he liked most about me was that I'd heard his stories less often than the rest of the party. I must also have developed a successful expression while he was telling them, because he evidently believed I was digesting every word; so I quite soon became a sort of holiday confidant. Added to which I was an experienced but uncompetitive fisherman, so I could occasionally give him a tip or even a helping hand which he could turn to his own credit when he reported the fortunes of the day to the others over dinner.

We were always first down to breakfast at the lodge. For me getting up early was a habit; for the Moor it was to enable the forces of gravity to disseminate the effects of the previous evening's alcohol more evenly away from his head. He would sit at the breakfast table sneezing and saying 'Bloody hell' at intervals, while I bent behind the copy of yesterday's *Times* which had come up the previous evening and served as shelter from his stormy blasts. Then, as the others started to come down, the daily ritual began of 'Good mornings' and questions about the weather which the Moor and I referred to as the 'dawn chorus'. This was not much to his taste, so he would hurry through his breakfast and then suggest to me that it was time to step outside to contemplate the day. And so we would make our escape.

On one such morning we were standing in front of the lodge assessing the prospects before adjourning to the fishing room to set ourselves up for the river. Something was on his mind.

'Don't know a bent doctor, do you?' he asked.

Of all the people in the household, I was probably his least likely bet. He must have been aware of that. I guessed this was something he wanted to keep away from his usual circle.

'I used to know one with one eye,' I replied, 'but that's about the only abnormality I've come across. Why do you ask?'

'Well,' said the Moor, 'I'm having a spot of argie-bargie with my golf club about using a buggy.'

'And...?'

'I want a certificate from a quack to say that I've got some disability that makes it inadvisable for me to walk round.'

'Have you?' I asked.

'Well, yes and no,' the Moor replied. 'I just feel a bit knackered at the end of a round, and I thought one of those buggies would save me a lot of trouble.'

'Well, I'm sure it would,' I said. 'So what's the problem?'

'The problem,' the Moor explained, 'is that the club doesn't allow them.'

'That is a problem,' I agreed. 'In fact it's almost a serious problem.'

The Moor took me into his confidence. His golf club – in common with many, let it be said – had a policy of not allowing players to drive round on buggies. I suppose they didn't want the dodgem-happy fraternity turning the fairways into the Somme. The Moor, however, quite liked the idea of forgoing the legwork. He asked the secretary one day at the bar and the secretary said, very sorry, no go.

Then why, said the Moor, did Teddy Garstang go round in one?

The secretary said that Teddy Garstang was a special case. He was an ex-president of the club and he had no legs. He balanced all right on the artificials but you couldn't expect him to stride round like a marathon man.

The Moor scented favouritism. What was the difference,

he asked with some edge, between having no legs and two legs that didn't work properly?

'Numerically,' the secretary answered facetiously, 'two.'

The Moor didn't like that. 'Look here,' he said, 'this isn't a joke. I spend a fortune in this place. You're paid to look after your members.'

'Just write in formally,' the secretary suggested, 'and I'll ask the committee to consider it. But I don't think you'll get anywhere.'

The Moor took him metaphorically by the lapel. 'If I don't,' he said, 'you may feel the draught of democracy. If the rest of us are walking, we'll see how your precious ex-president Garstang enjoys crawling round on all twos.'

'Steady on,' said the secretary, backing away. 'Just pop it down on paper, with some medical backup, and I'll see that it's looked at fairly.'

'You'd better,' the Moor said.

So that was the background.

'What happened next?' I asked.

He pulled two photocopied letters out of his jacket pocket and passed them to me.

The first letter was from the Moor.

At the suggestion of the secretary, may I make formal application to the committee to use a buggy when playing a round at the club. I am aware that as a matter of general policy the committee's decision is not to allow buggies except in special circumstances – specifically, in the case of Mr Garstang, who, I would be the first to agree, is an obviously deserving case. But now, as the days go by, I find myself in an increasingly arduous situation, with the result that I may shortly have to give up my membership if my application is not viewed sympathetically. I look forward to your confirmation that my use of the buggy will be in order.

The second letter was from the secretary on behalf of the committee.

The committee have carefully considered your request to use a buggy when playing at the club. They are unanimous in their feeling that the general wish of members is that buggies should not be allowed on the course except in very exceptional circumstances; and that the case of Mr Garstang meets those circumstances. We take your point that if there is a comparable case of physical handicap which would result in a long-serving member being obliged to abandon playing at the club if the services of a buggy were not available, this is something that must be considered on its merits. But you will appreciate that extremely stringent rules must be applied and only the most pressing and deserving cases considered, if we are not to relax the rules to the disadvantage of the membership as a whole.

May we therefore ask you to submit a suitable medical certificate endorsing your case and we promise to review the matter again to see whether we can reconcile your own special situation with the broader interests of the club.

He watched me get to the end.

'So I need a doctor to sign a paper saying I've got some appropriate ailment.'

'I know this will sound ingenuous,' I said, 'but the doctors I know aren't too keen about compromising themselves over a golf buggy. My father was a doctor. My oldest friend is still a doctor. These people are very out of date. They have quaint ideas about professional integrity.'

The Moor looked surprised. 'But all he's got to do is pop his monicker on the bottom of the paper. We can put down the medical details. Couldn't we find something in *Black's Medical Dictionary*?'

'They won't want to sign it if it's not true.'

He looked suddenly impatient. 'But they must often be signing things that aren't true.'

'I think they suppose them to be true at the time they're signing.'

'You take a very trusting view of the world,' the Moor said.

'I've had a sheltered life. There was a doctor once, I seem to remember, who practised in the waiting room of one of the London railway termini. He might be your man, if he's still at large. He might even have kept some headed paper. Paddington Station's not quite Harley Street, but I shouldn't think the committee are that hot on their medical geography.'

The Moor laid a hand on my shoulder. 'Well, put on your thinking cap. Inspiration may come to you on the river.'

Inspiration did come – not quite on the river but as I was walking back to the lodge. It offered a solution which had the attraction of being apparently authentic without seriously compromising the integrity of the doctor who endorsed it.

I didn't see the Moor until just before dinner. He was sunk into an armchair drinking a martini. The rest of the party were present, so I didn't think it the moment to mention my plan. But as we went in to eat I was able to tell him that I'd had an idea and I'd tell him about it at breakfast before the others came down. He raised his eyebrows questioningly. I told him I thought it would work.

What we had to do was prepare a statement which ascribed to the Moor a condition of extreme indolence which made him too lazy to play a round without the services of a buggy. This condition we would call perissarhathumia, a compound from the Greek adjective 'perissos', meaning overmuch, and the Greek noun 'rhathumia', meaning indolence. The Moor's doctor, with only a litle

[44]

prompting, would probably sign such a statement – it was only the naming of the condition that was devious. It also seemed unlikely that the committee would penetrate its disguise. With a touch of medical authority, the Moor would be unlucky not to be motorised.

Before I came down in the morning I wrote out the following statement:

> Mr Gervase Marston complains of symptoms of a condition which might be defined as perissarhathumia, which would make him unlikely to undertake a round of golf should he be denied the services of a buggy.

This, according to the Moor himself, seemed broadly true.

As the two of us sat down to breakfast, the dawn chorus not yet started, I passed him the sheet of paper.

'This might do the trick,' I said. 'It's not inviting your doctor to perjure himself. Nor is it, if you consider it carefully, a medical certificate. But it might bamboozle the committee.'

'That wouldn't take much doing,' the Moor said, taking the statement from me.

I waited with some anxiety as he read it.

He beamed. 'It looks perfect,' he said. 'What a wonderful-sounding disease. Is it something disgusting?'

'No,' I said, 'it's just another name for an inclination to put your feet up. The Greeks, as usual, had a word for it. Two words in this case.'

'It's amazing what olive oil and sandals can do for your vocabulary,' the Moor said reflectively.

I didn't think it an observation that caught the true spirit of the classical tradition, but I kept my reservations to myself. He didn't press me further on perissarhathumia. If he was proposing to do so, he was baulked by the beginning of the dawn chorus. The daily ritual was upon us.

We parted company at the end of the week, heading south

separately but maintaining the conspiracy by telephone. Before long the Moor's doctor rang me about the statement and sportingly agreed to participate. He apparently reassured his patient that a lack of activity was not the same thing as an inability to be active. The Moor looked at him rather strangely and said this was something he already knew. A letter was sent to the committee with another formal application for the services of a buggy and we settled back for the response.

It came about a fortnight later, a letter from the secretary that read as follows:

> The committee met to discuss your application on 26 July and I am happy to inform you that the services of a buggy will be available to you whenever you wish to play at the club. The committee have asked me to express our concern and sympathy at your indisposition and hope that it will not prevent you from enjoying many more years of active membership.

'Bob's your uncle,' said the Moor.

In fact, as someone who had been present later confided, the committee meeting had been less serene than the secretary's letter suggested.

When the secretary had come to item 4 on the agenda – 'A letter from Mr Gervase Marston applying for leave to use a buggy' – the mood around the table was hardly receptive. Wing Commander Dazeley said if you asked him (which nobody had), Marston was a confounded pest. It was known that the Wing Commander didn't like the way the Moor addressed him as 'Biggles', but that shouldn't have been allowed to prejudice the rights and wrongs of item 4.

'I don't understand these people,' he went on. 'What's golf if it isn't exercise?'

'A game?' suggested someone. 'Relaxation?'

'What's Marston got to relax from?' the Wing Commander

wanted to know. 'He's never done a stroke of work in his life.'

'Aren't we rather prejudging the issue?' asked Mr Schofield, who tended not to fly close formation with the Wing Commander if it could be avoided. Everybody reluctantly agreed that they needed the Wing Commander on the committee because he actually enjoyed doing all the organisational things that nobody else could face. But he didn't make you laugh much.

Mr Beck, the chairman, agreed with Mr Schofield. He thought they ought to see what Marston had to say. He asked the secretary to read out the letter.

The secretary did so. He then acquainted them with the medical evidence, which took a lot of wind out of their tyres. There was a long silence as they looked at each other.

'What's whatever it is?' the chairman asked eventually.

'As I understand it,' replied Mr Ellis-Saul, who was the closest you get to a polymath on golf club committees, which isn't usually very close, 'it's a sort of clinical enervation.'

'What's wrong with that?' the chairman said. 'Half the members suffer from that.'

'I think we should look at this seriously,' the secretary said. 'Mr Marston can be difficult, but he's pretty popular.'

'He's also fairly generous,' the chairman reminded them.

'With his wife's money,' added the aeronautical killjoy.

'Well, it all counts,' the chairman said. 'But if we say yes to Marston, won't it trigger a barrage of applications from all the other walking wounded?'

'If it does, they'll have to keep walking,' the secretary said flatly. 'I think we should allow Mr Marston the buggy if we've done the same for Mr Garstang.'

'But Teddy's got no legs,' the committee protested.

'According to this', the secretary said, waving the doctor's certificate, 'Mr Marston's aren't exactly first choice for the *entrechat*.'

'He looked all right when I saw him last,' the chairman said. 'He said he was off salmon fishing.'

Wing Commander Dazeley looked suddenly triumphant. 'Yes,' he said, 'how does he expect to catch salmon if his legs are so dodgy?'

'Perhaps he uses a rod,' Mr Schofield said, and the snigger that greeted his remark reminded the Wing Commander that much of the committee was ranged against his habitual disapproval. It could be as key a factor in the vote on the buggy as the Moor's incipient perissarhathumia.

'I think he's an idle layabout,' he said severely, closing for the prosecution, 'and if his legs are too bad for golf he should take up tiddlywinks.'

The secretary saw a danger there.

'If we tell him that,' he said, 'he might get his wife to buy the club and we'd all be taking up tiddlywinks.'

'Let's vote on it,' the chairman said.

The Moor won by a single vote. The secretary was instructed to write a cordial letter giving him the good news. The Wing Commander looked very displeased. His own unpopularity was bad enough; it was intolerable that it should work obliquely in favour of the Moor.

The Moor used the second of the club buggies and pronounced it too slow. Mrs Marston then bought him one for a birthday present which went four times as fast. Club observers reckoned that a collision between Garstang in the club transport and the Moor in his Links Mustang was odds on within a year, with the event quickly becoming unbackable as the more alert punters realised that the crash was likely to be deliberate rather than accidental. But the punters lost their money. There was no collision.

There are factors in this story that make one wonder whether even within the internal politics of golf club life there could be a scheme of things. The committee polymath,

Mr Ellis-Saul, rumbled the Moor. He arrived at the derivation of perissarhathumia and guessed that it described a straightforward moral inadequacy rather than a bona fide medical condition. If so, the committee's acceptance of it made them look very silly indeed. He began to match his suspicions to some artful observation of the Moor and grew steadily more convinced that a wilful deception had taken place. But he found himself in a dilemma. As one of the members of the committee, he resented being regarded by the Moor as a buffoon. It was not the slight on the committee that he minded – in his opinion 'buffoon' was a fair description of several of them – but the personal affront was hard to take. He wanted to establish with the Moor that he wasn't personally deceived, but he didn't want the passing of this information to escalate into a confrontation between the Moor and the likes of Wing Commander Dazeley. If that happened, everybody would be made to look completely ridiculous and the newspapers – it was socially a smart club – would have a field day.

Mr Ellis-Saul eventually decided to take Mr Beck into his confidence – not in Mr Beck's capacity as chairman of the club committee, though that was a factor, but as a sensible friend. He told Mr Beck his findings and explained his position. He wanted some moral supremacy asserted over the Moor without handing him over to the likes of the aeronautical killjoy. Mr Beck agreed with him about the killjoy, but then started getting dreadfully responsible and speaking of his obligations to the club. A scandal, he agreed, was not in the general interest, but there was a principle involved. He should take the matter up with the Moor and demand his resignation.

Mr Ellis-Saul read the matter differently. He was fairly sure that the Moor would believe he could make a joke of the matter if the committee tried to expel him. The committee members would wind up looking much sillier than he did. It was he after all who had duped them, not the other way round. The other members of the club would believe that the committttee had mishandled the affair and any move to expel the Moor, who was very popular, would almost certainly be resisted. He meanwhile would simply surrender his rights to the buggy and make a public joke of the committee for their gullibility in allowing him the buggy in the first place.

In the face of this policy conundrum, Mr Ellis-Saul and Mr Beck did the obvious thing. Nothing. They procrastinated, keeping their information to themselves, while the Moor continued happily with his charade.

Some weeks later Mr Beck took Mr Ellis-Saul aside in the clubhouse and said he'd been thinking. Mr Ellis-Saul invited his friend to tell him more. Mr Beck said he thought they should let the Moor know he wasn't fooling them and treat the matter entirely dismissively. They should say they weren't involving the committee, or even asking him to give up the buggy; they simply regarded it as an obvious, childish but no more than regrettable practical joke.

Mr Ellis-Saul said this was the voice of wisdom. Mr Beck looked pleased and a game was set up between the Moor and Mr Ellis-Saul and Mr Beck and Mr Garstang, in the course of which the Moor would be cut down to size. Once again, however, the initiative was wrested away from the forces of retribution because of the incident, on the very day of the match, involving the Moor and Squaddy, the secretary's dog.

The Moor was always careful within the precincts of the club to maintain the impression of being a perissarhathumiac. He developed some telling grimaces, and occasionally stooped to press a hand to his knee when he saw the secretary in the clubhouse. On the morning in question, however, he forgot himself completely. He was getting his clubs out of the boot of his car when Squaddy, an odious

'The secretary snatched up Squaddy . . .'

short-haired creature to whom the secretary was obsessively devoted, ran up and removed from the front seat a large slice of quiche that the Moor had brought with him for lunch. The dog then dived under the car and began to eat the quiche, while the Moor shouted at it from a horizontal position on the gravel. When this did no good, he drew a 2 iron out of his bag and began to thrash it under the car, at the same time raising his voice to such an extent that the secretary, hearing the commotion, came to the window of his office, just in time to see Squaddy shoot out on three legs from between the Moor's back wheels, having evidently sustained a sharp rap in the slats from the head of the 2 iron.

The animal's yelping tore at the secretary's heart. Incensed, he pitched out of the clubhouse and closed on the Moor, who was getting to his feet beside the car. The secretary snatched up Squaddy and turned for home again with the dog under his arm, shouting invective at the Moor as he ran. The Moor, now equally incensed and forgetting the need to feign his condition, vigorously pursued him, probably not to inflict physical injury on the secretary or even his dog, but certainly to make offensive statements about them both.

The secretary reached the safety of his office just far enough in front of the Moor to get the door closed and locked. He set the dog gently down on the floor, where it turned upside down and started some rather theatrical yelping. It was in no position to get its own back: such powers of retaliation as came naturally to it were thwarted by the locked office door, through the keyhole of which the Moor was about to address them. The secretary therefore carried the responsibility for both of them. He decided that he wouldn't put the matter to committee – he would immediately withdraw the buggy facilities. The Moor's disability seemed too intermittent to warrant special privileges. He informed the Moor of this through the keyhole of the office door.

The Moor, kneeling to direct his voice simultaneously through the keyhole from the other side, tendered his resignation and added a few personal hopes for the secretary's future and a further hope, more strongly expressed, that Squaddy wouldn't have one. At this, singing the repeated lyric 'perissarhathumia' to the tune of the Red Flag, he walked out of the clubhouse. Mr Beck and Mr Ellis-Saul, assembled for the match, watched in consternation.

The chairman wrote that on behalf of the committee he accepted the Moor's resignation with regret. He then privately got in touch with the Moor and reported that he and Mr Ellis-Saul were perfectly aware of the deceit he had played on the club, and should he vindictively try to discomfort them now that he had resigned, they would ensure that his name festered in clubland where the notion of dishonour was still used as a weapon of social discrimination.

I heard the Moor's account of all this the following year up on the Dee, twice; and I'd heard it on the telephone before. It was that week that I fell and hurt my hip out fishing. I accepted the medical description of my condition and the Moor made up nothing to embellish it, as I had done for him. Just as well perhaps: the profession should be allowed to devise its own vocabulary. Meanwhile I see no entry for perissarhathumia in the medical reference books. We must assume that the condition is either not acknowledged or else it has attacked the chroniclers of medical advance and left them too indolent to record it.

4
Winning Ways

I knew it must be the bursar when the telephone rang. He had a sixth sense about inconvenience. Helen was out and I'd just spilt golden syrup over the dog. I picked up the receiver, put my hand over the mouthpiece, and warned the dog that if it moved one inch, it was curtains. I was wrong. It was chair covers – it took a quick circuit of the room rubbing against them, then started rolling over and over on the carpet.

'They tell me you've taken up golf,' the bursar was saying.

'They probably haven't told you how I've got on,' I said.

'No, I've been hearing nothing but good reports. Are you accepting challenges?' he asked. 'You've been dodging playing with me for years.'

I made a non-committal sound I'd perfected in communications with the bursar. It was delivered with the mouth closed, too short and high-pitched to be thought a groan, but equally not hinting at enthusiasm.

He interpreted it, as usual, in the way that suited him. He knew it was a long haul from Dorset to East Sussex but why didn't I bring a partner, come and stay overnight and we'd have a round, or possibly two? Alternatively, he could come over to me. He sounded a little hesitant about that, which would have pleased Helen.

It was a nettle that would have to be grasped at some stage, so I accepted in principle for the away match and said I'd confirm the details when I'd had a word with Tiger.

Tiger had been an East Sussex man and he was still a member of Royal St George's, Sandwich. It was one of the courses very much on our agenda, and although it was a shame to blight it with the bursar, it seemed the obvious place if we had to go in that direction anyway. I explained to Tiger about the bursar. Would he help me out?

'You bet,' he said.

'No, you bet,' I corrected him. 'This man's a wily customer. He's not cannon fodder like Eric and Deric.'

'We'll sort him out,' Tiger said.

When Tiger said that, he made you believe it was true.

The bursar sent a postcard confirming the arrangements. He was looking forward to meeting Tiger, he said, and the fourth would be Sir Geoffrey Wrexham, who was a member at Prince's, over the way from St George's, where we might play our afternoon round. I was obviously expected to know about Sir Geoffrey Wrexham but I'd never heard of him. Tiger hadn't heard of him either. He said he'd ask around. His enquiries established that Sir Geoffrey was something to do with accountancy and looked like a heron. It wasn't a comprehensive briefing, but it was all we had. Someone remembered that his detractors called him 'Wrexham by name and Wrexham by nature', but we didn't think that added much. People who made jokes like that deserved to be financially outmanoeuvred – which is presumably why they were detractors.

When the bursar had suggested that we 'come and stay overnight', I had ingenuously supposed that he was offering us hospitality. It was apparent from his postcard, however, that he was expecting us to find our own accommodation in the neighbourhood. I reported this to Tiger somewhat apologetically on the telephone, but he sounded delighted and said we could go and stay with his friends the Unwins. Tiger seemed to have oases of hospitality all over the country.

The Unwins claimed to be delighted too, so Tiger and I drove over together and stayed the night with them about twelve miles from Sandwich. They had a big old farmhouse, decorator-pickled to discipline the antiquity and upgrade the comfort. It was a cradle of domestic and cultural serenity, with little piles of books and magazines all over the place and sonorous classical music that came on and off like a thermostat. The Unwins themselves were handsome and devoted, with two confident young children who were trained to say goodnight to adults so winningly that you almost wished they weren't going to bed. It all put you in a good mood.

I hadn't been teaching at Combermere for a lifetime without getting to know the sunlit classes. The loud ones and the quiet ones are really just the same model being driven at different speeds. It's a question of whether you'd rather have the showing off or the conspicuous self-effacement. The Unwins were the latter and that undoubtedly makes for the better overnight stay – if you're just there for the accommodation. They had good wine, and mineral water and biscuits beside your bed and all the perfumes of Arabia and a good few from Floris in the bathroom. And if the whole package was obviously received taste, it was received from people who knew about comfort. We went to bed in excellent spirits and Mr Unwin asked us two or three times whether there was anything else we'd like, and apologised another two or three times that he'd be off to the train before we were up but Deirdre would look after us – 'Won't you, darling'. And Deirdre said 'Of course, darling' and they went through a ritual of locking up and turning out the lights and the world seemed just momentarily a better place for all this well-heeled civility.

When we came down in the morning Mr Unwin, as predicted, had left for the train and Deirdre had come up trumps with the breakfast – scrambled eggs and all the rest in silver dishes with terribly hot lids, and a deck of jams and marmalades and that maximum-trouble coffee that one longs for other people to produce. The tablecloth was spotless, the silver gleaming, the choice of newspapers staidly comprehensive. I felt myself settling into the emotional equivalent of very expensive sheets. It was too early in my retirement for me to have mastered the art of pottering – I still found it difficult to invest inactivity with a sense of purpose – but extended meals are good high ground from which to contemplate one's plans. It was Tiger who looked at his watch and said we should be getting on our way.

Deirdre nannied us out to the car and gave Tiger a farewell embrace, then shook hands with me and said how much she hoped I'd come again. We got into the car and I wound down my window in case she came round my side, but she didn't – she framed her pretty face in Tiger's open window and beamed us both a lateral goodbye.

'She's a good girl, Deirdre,' Tiger said, as we drove much too fast down towards the gate, waving as we went. You couldn't deny it.

We were due at St George's at 10 a.m. The bursar met us outside the clubhouse and greeted us effusively. I watched him getting Tiger's measure, heard him say how he and I went back a long way, typically trying to demote Tiger's friendship with me below his own. But the bursar and I weren't really friends, we were two people bonded by the shared benign experience of Combermere. We could exchange so many happy memories that after a spell apart we could almost believe that some of them were of each other. But, from my side anyway, I don't think they were. That's not to say we were enemies; perhaps competitors is more the right word.

It wasn't long before Sir Geoffrey Wrexham appeared. The description of him as looking like a heron wasn't far out. He had a long thin nose and his hair had receded so far that you didn't know whether the centre was coming forward or the sides were going back. He was very tall and spare and was constantly looking about him as if in fear of attack.

The bursar effected the introductions. Sir Geoffrey pointed his forefinger to and fro between the bursar and myself.

'Am I right in thinking that you're old friends from Combermere?'

I let the bursar answer that one.

'You'll have known Henry Cholderton,' Sir Geoffrey thought.

Henry Cholderton had been headmaster of Combermere for twenty-nine of the years I had taught there. Some knowledge of him was inevitable. There were only nine of us on the staff.

'Very much so,' I said.

It occurred to me that Sir Geoffrey was rummaging in his memory for old boys of his acquaintance. This could go on all morning. I looked imploringly at Tiger, who intervened to ask if Sir Geoffrey knew the course.

'Yes, I've played it many times,' he said. Then he lowered my morale by telling me you needed to be handy with the driver. If the carries at some holes were as Sir Geoffrey indicated, my short and straight technique was in for a bruising; it would be up to Tiger to keep us alive. At the eighth and the twelfth you had to carry a ridge that I normally wouldn't try to get to first or second bounce. And on the holes where I might still be in play when it came to the second shot, there were so many bunkers that the place looked like a gigantic gruyère.

'I hear you're very straight off the tee,' the bursar said as we got our trolleys together.

'It sounds as if you need length as well,' I said.

[58]

'Yes,' the bursar conceded, 'it can be a bit tricky in a wind. But the wind's not too bad today.'

I was relieved to hear it wasn't too bad. There were no trees by which to measure its strength from the moving branches. I hoped it hadn't blown them all away.

Tiger and I had agreed that he'd shoulder the bets, but that we'd pretend we were dividing them between us. If we lost, the bursar wouldn't want me to escape scot free. He must have been delighted with our choice of venue. You couldn't imagine anywhere more likely to take its toll of the weaknesses in my game and Sir Geoffrey was certainly not on parade solely for what the bursar might regard as social cachet (though that would have mattered to him too).

None of this was a surprise to me. If the day went badly, at least I could generate some annoyance by not seeming to mind. But I knew the bursar's meaner instincts sometimes served him poorly; there was a backfire factor always in his schemes. It sustained one's faith in Headquarters. I hoped their winged representative would be on the *qui vive* today.

After one or two anaemic tee shots when it was my turn to drive, I began to have my doubts. The bursar's jubilant cries of 'Bad luck' were so larded with insincerity and Sir Geoffrey was playing with such chilling concentration, as if every shot were a column of figures, that I feared we were in for a drubbing. But no, we all soon realised that we'd caught Tiger on a good day. I'd found in the past his direction could be a little wayward, but now he was booming them away with his woods and irons, full of confidence, talking his head off and clearly beginning to unsettle Sir Geoffrey. I helped us to a couple of short holes by outputting the bursar and, to my agreeable surprise, we had our heads in front at the turn.

The twelfth has a diagonal carry off the tee. The bursar and Tiger both made it over the ridge to the fairway. I played rather a cautious second, while Sir Geoffrey thumped into a deep bunker just short of the green, leaving a horrible lie for the bursar.

We left him to make the best of it in the bunker and went on to the green up ahead of him. Tiger and I fancied our chances for the hole, reckoning that the bursar would do well to get the ball clear of the sand, let alone anywhere near the pin. We couldn't see him from where we were standing and there was some delay before he finally played. But then the ball sailed up to finish in the heart of the green.

He'd known that we couldn't see him make his shot – or, before he made it, scoop his ball back to an easy lie. Nor did it occur to any of us that he'd cheated; we all spontaneously congratulated him on what seemed an exceptionally skilful shot, considering how high up the face of the bunker the ball had lodged. It was particularly bad luck that his misdemeanour was observed by a man who was coming up from the beach; and even worse luck that the man stopped to ask me the best way up to the main road as we went over to the thirteenth tee. We had a brief conversation: I remember asking him whether the sea was cold and he said he'd have been in trouble without a blowlamp. Then he nodded in the direction of the bursar, who was just walking on to the tee, and expressed the hope, with a broad smile, that I was playing with the man who'd done 'a huge cheat in the bunker'.

My feelings were not of reproach for the bursar's dishonesty but of vindictive elation that it had come to my attention. I don't suggest this was a creditable reaction, but I think most will understand it. He'd been obnoxiously cocky as Sir Geoffrey holed the easy putt and heaped praises on him; he even asked if we were playing sandies, which he knew we weren't. (No, I didn't know what they were either, but they're bets on holing out in two from a bunker.) Now I kept my counsel. Silently, I thanked Headquarters and said I'd take the matter on from there.

It was now almost essential for me to finish on the losing

'A *huge* cheat in the bunker.'

side – the bursar's odiousness in victory was something in itself that needed to be punished. So when Tiger's game, obligingly, began to fray and we found ourselves slipping behind, there was for me a particular sweetness in our misfortune. The bursar's demeanour, superficially gracious, would have done no credit to a hobnailed boot. When we lost the last of the byes on the eighteenth to an excellent four and Sir Geoffrey laid a congratulatory arm around his shoulders, I felt for an anxious moment that should Sir Geoffrey withdraw the arm the bursar might disintegrate from the inner forces of self-esteem. He looked across at me with an expression of take-that supremacy. I looked as deflated as one can on cloud three over par.

I had been rehearsing in my mind the way in which I would administer the *coup de grâce*. I decided not to discredit him in front of Sir Geoffrey and Tiger; the nuances of our relationship didn't concern them and I wasn't setting up as a moral tribunal. Anyway Tiger had fairly lost his bets, with the possible exception of the errant twelfth. My own losses, which came to £6, were cheap at the price.

Tiger paid Sir Geoffrey, I settled with the bursar. I allowed him, in the circumstances, a generous period of self-congratulation. It was only when we were going into the club-house for lunch and I was following close behind him that I quietly told him he'd shocked the man who was coming up from the beach.

He checked and turned to face me. I could see him trying to steady himself as the implications of my remark struck home. I'd thought his only escape would have been to try to laugh it off, but given the years of our relationship we both knew that what was being exposed was his insecurity, his need to win. For me, of all people, to have exposed it must have been very painful.

The preparatory school world in which we had lived had an established morality, based broadly on what you could and couldn't do in the estimation of your peers. The boys at Combermere weren't out, in the main, to 'beat the system'; they were following a code of conduct that had been handed down from the days when boys like them had gone out to run an empire. We encouraged this morality: it was broadly defensible, it was clearly defined and it gave the staff an easier time; it was still some time before the boys grew up, went out to run the empire and found it wasn't there. We encouraged loyalty to school and good manners; sometimes, when dealing with the headmaster's mother, they were more or less the same thing, and both a strain. In our over-simplified little world, cheating at golf was something you'd never do. In the real world, I suspect, it was less of a novelty.

The bursar looked quickly over his shoulder at Tiger and Sir Geoffrey who were going on ahead. There was something suddenly pathetic in his concern and in the way he turned back to face me in total capitulation.

'I'll keep it to myself,' I reassured him.

He muttered his thanks. There was so much that had gone between us, over such a long time, that explanations or ex-cuses were of no avail. It seemed to both of us a final sorry verdict on our acquaintance.

Our plan had been to have a second round at Prince's after lunch. It was apparent, however, that the bursar was dis-tinctly out of sorts.

'I'm really sorry,' he said, 'but I'm not sure I'm up to a second round.'

'Have your winnings gone to your head?' Sir Geoffrey asked genially, pulling his beak out of a glass of beer.

The bursar didn't answer; but he and I knew they'd hit him a lot lower than that.

We finished our lunch. The others kept glancing at me in concern for the bursar's loss of form. I tried to project a look that told them not to worry, but my facial semaphore may have been mistranslated when I unexpectedly struck chutney in my beef sandwich. So they may have suspected that something was gravely wrong; or perhaps that whatever was wrong with the bursar had already got to me, and might at any moment attack them too across the table. The conversation, if one could call it that, proceeded in slow lobs until the bursar stood up, apologised, and said he'd better be getting home. I said we'd give him a hand with his clubs.

We saw him to his car. 'Are you sure you'll be all right?' Sir Geoffrey asked.

Yes, the bursar said, he was quite sure; and he drove away. He and I made no further contact; I'm sure he felt himself disgraced.

With the bursar having dropped out, the plan for a fourball at Prince's was somewhat compromised but we went along anyway. I'd steeled myself for a marathon and I wasn't going to give up now.

Dave Marr once said, so Tiger told me, that you should never bet with anyone you meet on the first tee who has a deep suntan, a one iron in his bag and squinty eyes. So we had no reason to mistrust the stranger who joined us for the afternoon round. He didn't offend on the suntan test, there was no sign of an accomplice with a parasol, he didn't have a one iron, and his gaze had the integrity of a television evangelist reading a cue card. He interposed himself apologetically with another member, who'd apparently been playing with him in the morning and had to go. They saw we were an odd number and were looking somewhat hesitant, so it seemed reasonable to ask whether we were waiting for someone or were indeed one short. I suppose, in retrospect it had all the characteristics of the classic sting, but Sir Geoffrey gave him a visual audit and said, yes, why not. He introduced himself. His name was Courtenay Wadsworth.

We spun for partners. Courtenay and I came down heads. Tiger asked whether we'd care for an interest in the result.

Yes, said Courtenay, he was game. I said rather diffidently that I wasn't really a punter, and Courtenay said not to worry, he'd carry the bets for our side. Tiger looked really pleased and they started agreeing the bets. There was obviously an overall stake on the result, but you could press the bet if you were two down. Tiger piled on the suggestions – closest to pin, sandies, fewest putts; each time Courtenay nodded his agreement. It was four ball, best ball. And we were off.

Looking back, I can see that Courtenay's misfortunes on the early holes were skilfully contrived. We went four down; he pressed the bets in an appealingly cavalier way, shrugging and saying with a smile, 'What's money?', although the answer to his rhetorical question, as it turned out, was something that he was extremely shrewd at acquiring. Mysteriously he began to find his form, apologising for what seemed to be flukes, kissing his driver as if there were a degree of luck in the way he rifled the ball off the tee, and expressing surprise when Tiger totted up the state of the bets at the thirteenth and found we were £90 in front. 'It can't last,' he said. Tiger believed him and pressed again.

It was a rout and very nearly worse. Courtenay had a quite gettable putt on the eighteenth that had so many complicated bets riding on it that even Sir Geoffrey would have had to calculate them on the back of his card. He fractionally misjudged the line. Or did he intentionally miss? The show of gracious failure seemed so spontaneous and sportsmanlike that it would take a cynic to mistrust it; or perhaps a realist. Tiger and Sir Geoffrey were so relieved at their final let off that they actually commiserated with Courtenay, although he had unburdened them of perhaps £150 each. They paid up cheerfully, Courtenay bought us all drinks in the clubhouse and offered some plain philosophy about the vagaries of Dame Fortune. I couldn't help feeling that it was all a little too good to be true and I've no doubt he was a very accomplished player indeed. Tiger and Sir Geoffrey didn't want to believe that, even if it entered their heads. They made their goodbyes to him in the warmest terms and even said to each other afterwards what a sporting competitor he was.

When we got back to St George's the afternoon had receded into early evening. We stood with our drinks, looking benevolently over the area of our day's exertions. This is land once surrendered by the sea. Not everybody wants a windswept vista of geological acne – the sea apparently included – but golfers' requirements are fortunately a special case. The appeal of the links course is that, being exposed, it's a creature of moods; its challenge to the golfer varies dramatically according to wind and weather, and this quirky unpredictability takes the clockwork out of even the professional game. There isn't, frankly, much clockwork about mine and I'm not that keen on having what there is blasted backwards by a Force 9 gale. So if I'm ever prompted to quote what Bernard Darwin wrote about St George's – that it was 'as nearly my idea of heaven as is to be attained on any earthly links' – on a rough day I'd emphasise the word 'links' rather than the word 'earthly'; which is to say not very near. In fact not very near at all if you throw in the likes of the bursar.

But today we'd been extended rather than routed by the course, and with the evening sun putting a sparkle into Pegwell Bay I could see why St George's retained such an allure among the *cognoscenti*. These celebrated courses have their own mythology of triumph and disaster, and although I'd read about the great moments of St George's it's different when you've played the course yourself and you're in there with the ghosts. Glancing at my card and comparing it with Henry Cotton's opening two rounds of 67 and 65 in the 1934 Open, I could understand why Uncle Reggie had only taken on Cotton at canasta. What's more, these are stories you have to believe. Golfers are unlike fishermen in this respect; they're almost as bad at repeating the same story *ad nauseam*, but they're less prone to exaggeration because golf is a game of precise distances and recorded scores. You can't convincingly boast about the one that got away. So if you're just an ordinary player, your only short cut to the hall of fame is through the freak achievement – like killing two caddies with one ball, or having your cap snatched off by a raven. I believe there is a case of a golfer being transfixed by his own broken club, and probably many cases of golfers being spliced by their own mainbrace; but I'm content to settle for anonymity in the record books.

At St George's the idiosyncrasies of the terrain are at the heart of the course's appeal. They not only make for constant interest but also give you an unexpected sense of privacy. I imagine that swimming round Cape Horn would give you a comparable feeling of eventful shelter, although St George's isn't quite so tiring and probably the one fate that won't overtake you there is drowning.

'What an evening,' Sir Geoffrey said, breaking the mellow silence. He pointed across Pegwell Bay. 'Look at Ramsgate.'

He didn't mean that. It was a remark about visibility, not about the look of the town. He was asking us to note how the white cliffs round the town stood out in the clarity of the light.

'I once went to Ramsgate on a motor bike,' Tiger recalled. This was ribbon development conversation. 'There was a fair, I remember, and we went on the dodgems. Haven't been there since. That must have been a few years ago.'

Sir Geoffrey, to my relief, didn't offer us any updates on Ramsgate. Instead he consulted his watch and thought we'd better be heading for home. If he thought that, with the heronry close by, it was certainly true for Tiger and me who had to get back to Dorset. It also nudged Tiger out of his

Ramsgate reverie. He stirred suddenly like a man lying back in the bath.

Sir Geoffrey said he'd ring the bursar and make sure he was all right. He shook his head. 'Very unlike him to pack in like that.'

I said I'd give him a call too, not because I intended to but because I guessed that was what Sir Geoffrey was expecting me to say. Then Tiger and I got our things together and loaded them into the car. Sir Geoffrey came across to say goodbye.

'Thanks very much,' he said. 'That was fun.'

I could agree with him; oddly, because I didn't associate Sir Geoffrey with that word. He was, personally, not fun; he seemed to me emotionally over-audited and, given half a chance, he'd talk to you about business. When people talk to me about business I feel the non-comprehension warning light beaming out of my forehead. But they go on talking. I suspect they're not telling me about business, but that they know about business. So I found myself apologising on the way home about uncongenial companions – Sir Geoffrey and the bursar were a choice combination.

'They've much in common with a bad lie,' Tiger said. 'They inhibit you.'

If you're the bursar, I thought, there's an answer to that.

5
Miranda

The original bond between Barnaby Reynolds and Rodney Coghlan was that they had twice been dismissed by employers in the City of London on the same day. This, and the fact that no further employers could be found to give them a chance of a third coincidence, prompted them to join forces in the financial consultancy of Reynolds Coghlan Associates Ltd, operating from three locations on the South Coast.

I met them through Tiger – Mrs Barnaby was Mrs Tiger's sister (and later our informant about the sorry tale that follows) – and we all had a round or two of golf together. They were both competent players – Barnaby about ten handicap, Rodney perhaps twelve – and quite congenial company in their way. I think, however, if I had been required to take their advice I should have preferred it to be about golf than about investments. Quite apart from their earlier employment record in the Square Mile, there is something rather defeatist about financial consultants who have offices close to steep cliffs.

The course near the coast where Barnaby and Rodney played most of their golf had a tempting hut on the ninth, where you could take in sustenance and make a telephone call to the office to say you were held up in a meeting. Not that Barnaby and Rodney, being in partnership, normally lied to each other about their business; but their social calendar occasionally needed diplomatic presentation. And the interest of both of them, along with numerous other male members of the club, was caught by the arrival at the hut of Miranda, a brunette who put out that she was twenty-six but was suspected of having completed a few unrecorded circuits in excess of that. She was what husbands called a nice cheerful girl and wives didn't.

Her presence at the hut added almost twenty minutes to the time of the average round and a new tendency to practise in the evening on the far side of the course, although there was a perfectly adequate practice ground behind the clubhouse. The takings at the hut rose spectacularly. The reason for this was not something in the soup but something in the service. Miranda herself, who remained resolutely unavailable off duty, bloomed on the good-humoured attentions of the golfers. The number of incoming telephone calls on a line normally reserved for outgoing untruths, doubled, then quadrupled, as she was propositioned with a degree of discretion from the car phones or, furtively, the clubhouse. The pigeon was well and truly among the cats.

Socially confident males at play don't always have a good effect on each other and there was a certain amount of sexist talk about the club's new acquisition and not a little speculation. This was not only regrettable in itself, but also unfair: if there was anything suggestive about Miranda, it wasn't she who was making the suggestions. Barnaby and Rodney, whose sense of refinement was vulnerable at the best of times, offended as much as most. Barnaby went so far as to bet Rodney that he could take Miranda with him on holiday, a bet which Rodney accepted, believing he could persuade her to go instead with him. The issue, *au fond*, was whether they were keeping the years at bay. They would talk bravely

'What husbands called a nice cheerful girl and wives didn't.'

about being as young as you feel, but the looking glass was beginning to be severe with them.

Their wives, who would also have had views on the wager, were not consulted. Both were ladies of strong character, quite pleasing appearance and more solid moral sinew than their husbands. Both ladies knew, from twenty years' experience, that their husbands had a tendency to be wayward. Their reactions to this were practical and confrontational; each wife had on occasion cut off all her husband's trousers at the knee, with the embroidered caveat set on the dressing table 'Being cheap can be expensive'. Yet, for all their matrimonial mettle, their influence was never wholly corrective, because Barnaby and Rodney colluded with each other. They allowed each other the indulgence of little 'business' trips, matched stories over evening engagements, and generally fought a joint rearguard action against their diminishing appeal. But now, for the first time in their long association, they were temporarily in competition.

For some reason Barnaby created a more favourable impression than Rodney in the pursuit of Miranda's company. Why either of them should have occupied her attention for longer than it took to pour out a drink or a bowl of soup is not easy to explain, since they were obvious marauders; but perhaps it was the novelty of Barnaby's approach. He affected an admiration for Miranda's cerebral qualities. It wasn't a line that had occurred to anyone else, but it seemed to work – probably because her cerebral qualities were not acute enough to detect that she was being subjected to an elaborate and extended stratagem.

One evening, just before some late practice, Barnaby immobilised her car. He watched while she closed up the hut and prepared to go home, then walked towards his car as she was making prolonged and unsuccessful efforts to start hers. He peered into the engine for her, confessed himself baffled (fortunately, so was she), then asked if he could give her a lift home, with the promise that he'd get someone along to locate the trouble and put it right. That would be more than kind, she said, but she didn't want to take him out of his way. No trouble, he assured her, he'd said he'd get some food on the way home as he'd be late after golf. Would she care to join him? Miranda, a little cautiously, agreed to this, reflecting that she'd have safely eaten the dinner by the time it was necessary to disappoint any more intimate plans that might occur to Barnaby for the continuation of the evening. So, fencing courtesies, they set off.

Miranda's conversational skills were fluent but not deep. She told Barnaby over the prawn cocktail that she liked astrology, skating and watching television. Oh yes, and she had a soft spot for horses.

'What sort of horses?' Barnaby asked.

She hesitated. 'All, really,' she said. 'Well, not clothes horses, but otherwise – you know, stuff you can ride. I like riding.'

It was no time for lofty thoughts. A bet was a bet. Barnaby struggled over this sparse conversational fare, attentive and a paragon of restraint. He told her he was hopeless at skating and he'd knocked over two people the only time he'd been to the Southampton rink. As for astrology, he knew there must be a lot in it; he'd always longed for someone to explain it clearly to him.

That was the invitation she needed. She babbled inconsequentially on and he contributed nods of appreciation and little smiles of understanding. At the end he said how easy it was now she explained it to him. Flattered, she wrongly thought him rather a gentleman.

He drove her home, wished her a most decorous goodnight, went back to the car park, resuscitated her car, arrived very early at the course the next morning, drove her car to her home, and accompanied her back to the club in it as she came in to work. When Rodney looked in the following evening for an hour's late practice, she coyly reported that Barnaby had been 'kindness itself'.

Rodney, knowing his man, was seriously put out. He struck twenty shots in succession with a 3 iron; and the gradual increment in the distance of each shot reflected the mounting competitive animosity he felt towards his partner. What was particularly disquieting was that Barnaby's honourable conduct, with him one of the surest signs of dishonourable intent, was being given credence. Rodney came off the practice ground in a state of irrational emotion and decided he would try there and then to win the bet. He went straight up to the hut and asked Miranda to come with him to Brittany. She pressed a strawberry flan into his face. He took her answer to be no.

Unknown to Rodney, Barnaby was having problems of his own. He was beginning to feel confident of winning the bet, but he was paying the price of progress. In affecting a long-term seduction strategy he had to paint a rather bleak picture of his married life. Miranda listened sympathetically to his fictions. She said she quite understood that they shouldn't be seen dining out together, and suggested she should cook him dinner in her flat when the coast was clear. This was a blow to Barnaby, who had hoped to eliminate rather than sideline their evening discussions on astrology and horses. He hoped that Miranda's flatmate, Val, might present an obstacle, but here again he was disappointed. Val, who worked during the day as a receptionist, went regularly to evening keep fit classes, which seemed to incapacitate her for everything except going to keep fit classes and eating chocolate biscuits under her desk at work. Towards the end of Miranda's illicit cuisine she would return to the flat wearing trainers and a track suit, and collapse into a chair with her eyes closed, sometimes to the accompaniment of very loud Caribbean music. This neither made her very good company, nor made her of use in fending off evenings of thin conversation unredeemed by carnal relations with Miranda.

Rodney of course knew none of this. He sensed however that Barnaby was making progress where he had failed and he waited with increasing resignation for his partner to claim his winnings. So when Barnaby announced he was going to Switzerland, the writing seemed to be on the wall, if not quite yet on the cheque.

It had always been the partners' practice to confide in each other about their business excursions, if only to maintain a front of collusion in the face of questions from other interested parties. On this occasion Rodney suspected that Barnaby wasn't telling *him* the truth, let alone anyone else. He asked the accountant to ring the firm's travel agent, asking for a copy invoice as they had mislaid the original. This elicited the information that Barnaby had paid for the tickets – in the plural – himself. A further call, supposedly on Barnaby's behalf, to check the flight number for someone who would be meeting the plane, revealed that Barnaby was headed for Nice. In the context of a solo trip to Switzerland, both Barnaby's arithmetic and his geography appeared to be at fault. Rodney was forced to think the unthinkable. It had to be Miranda. He decided not to question her directly but waited in a mood of resigned jealousy until Barnaby left on the Friday. On the Saturday he went to play golf. Tiger and I saw him outside the clubhouse and detected that he was in a state of agitation. He attributed it, with wider connnotations than we could appreciate, to his being left on his own by Barnaby.

When Rodney's four stopped at the hut Miranda was nowhere to be seen. Her substitute reported that she'd gone on holiday.

'Anywhere exotic?' Rodney asked.

'She didn't say.'

She didn't have to. Rodney thereupon decided to have Barnaby punished for succeeding where he had failed. It was after all a serious offence.

On the Monday he got his secretary to ring the travel agent and ask the flight number of Barnaby's plane from Nice next Friday – she had to arrange a car for him. The travel agent came up with the information.

That evening Rodney confided in his wife; or, to be more accurate, told Mrs Rodney something that she was sure to report to Mrs Barnaby, in spite of his disingenuous request that she should keep it to herself. As soon as he left for the office in the morning, Mrs Rodney rang up Mrs Barnaby to tell her that her husband was on holiday with the toothsome Miranda. This communiqué was received with cool detachment. After a few moments to collect her thoughts Mrs Barnaby decided that the least welcome spectacle with which her husband and Miranda would wish to be confronted would be a large party of his family and friends waiting at the barrier when BA 289 put down from Nice. Mrs Rodney was inclined to agree. She suggested that a band might add a touch of *je ne sais quoi* to the occasion. 'Yes,' said Mrs Barnaby, 'you're right. A band.' The tumbrils began to roll.

Mrs Barnaby found it surprisingly easy to muster twenty wellwishers to participate in her act of moral correction. Not only was she popular in her own right, but the exercise was seen in some quarters as a crusade, a declaration to other would be defaulters that the ranks of injured womanhood are a significant formation. There was to be no invective, Mrs Barnaby told her troops, only silent reproof. She then followed up Mrs Rodney's suggestion of a band, supplementing her posse with the cream of the local Silver. They would accompany Mrs Milne-Thomas, a broadshouldered local contralto who could bowl a choral bouncer with the best of them. The choice of anthem was 'Let the Bright Seraphim'.

Mrs Rodney, the informant, requested leave of absence. She assured Mrs Barnaby that both she and her husband were right behind her but preferred not to be in the party of confrontation. Some of the more militant wives thought this weak-kneed, but Mrs Barnaby recognised that the business partnership must not be prejudiced over a domestic issue. She further agreed to attribute the leak of information to the travel agents. To conclude the arrangements she hired half the fleet of Jack's Tours – one bus – and scheduled the expedition to arrive at Heathrow twenty minutes before the flight. This was one that Barnaby, not to mention the Airport Authority, wouldn't easily forget.

Rodney had every reason to feel a sly satisfaction. The responsibility for Barnaby's debacle wouldn't be laid at his door, and Miranda, who was obviously a lost cause, would be taught a lesson for preferring Barnaby's charms to his own. The moral wretchedness of his position was completely lost on him.

Halfway through Thursday afternoon, with all the arrangements made and the countdown, as it were, begun, there was an unnerving development. Barnaby's secretary reported that Barnaby had called, apparently from Lausanne, to say that everything had been going very well and that he was travelling back, as planned, with M. Ducros, who had arranged for a car to meet them at the airport. He had asked the secretary to pass on the message to his wife.

M. Ducros was a very rich Swiss who entrusted Barnaby with considerable commissions. He seemed in that respect to be lacking the financial acumen associated with so many of his countrymen. He was the only client to have followed Barnaby and Rodney when they left their City employers to set up on their own. In fact his intention was to demonstrate his annoyance with those employers over quite another

[77]

matter, although it seemed at the time a reckless way of expressing his displeasure. He was a man who wasn't very good at listening to advice – and so ideal for Barnaby and Rodney who weren't very good at giving it. Barnaby plied him with bonhomie and a fund of rather rude jokes which he didn't usually understand and, in an odd sort of way, the relationship prospered, although M. Ducros was much more useful to Barnaby and Rodney than they were to him.

That evening Mrs Barnaby rang up Mr and Mrs Rodney in a state of some concern. What did Rodney make of the latest development? Should the plan be called off? Moral issues aside, the last thing they wanted to do was to choke off the firm's best client. Rodney said he'd thought carefully about it all and his conclusion was that it was a bluff. It was just the sort of call, he said, that he'd have made in Barnaby's circumstances, although, he added hurriedly for the benefit of Mrs Rodney, he wasn't speaking from experience.

'So we press on?' said Mrs Barnaby.

'Definitely,' Rodney replied. 'Even supposing, by some totally remote chance, that Barnaby's telling the truth, the last thing he's going to do is to acknowledge that he knows any of you and so do us in with Ducros. We'll just have to come clean afterwards and say he was under suspicion.'

'Kiss and make up?'

'Precisely,' Rodney said. 'Your department.'

'Thanks,' said Mrs Barnaby.

The matter resolved, Rodney kept to his original plan of playing golf while Mrs Barnaby and the posse put the boot in at Heathrow. He was a little unsettled by Barnaby's call; but after going through it all again with his wife, he was reasonably sure that the advice he had given Mrs Barnaby was sound. If it wasn't, it would be more Mrs Barnaby's problem than their own. And that, they had to agree between themselves, made it sounder still.

His foursome teed off at nine o'clock the next morning. He'd telephoned the office to say he had a meeting in London, but he'd probably call mid-morning just to check everything was all right. He had in mind the telephone in the hut.

The quality of his game astonished everyone, not least himself. It must have been the exhilaration of revenge. By the time they reached the turn, he was apologising for his unusual form and he and his partner were six up. They went into the hut.

Whatever malicious powers may have infused Rodney's game on the outward half, the sight of Miranda preparing a Pimms No 1 summarily dispersed them.

She saw his look of surprise. She was giving nothing away. Their relationship, since the corrective application of the strawberry flan, had reverted to a wary civility.

'I thought you were out of the country,' he said.

'No,' she replied, 'I just popped up to the Lake District for a couple of days. My granny lives up there.'

Rodney stared at her in dismay. He glanced at his watch. The bus would have left for Heathrow. There was no stopping it now. He'd have to drive to the airport and call off the posse at the last moment. He could still make it if he set off in the next few minutes.

He'd already told his companions he'd have to make a telephone call. Now he pretended to make it. After a barely convincing interval he hurried back to them.

'Office crisis,' he said. 'I'm terribly sorry, but I'll have to go.'

The others tried to look concerned for his difficulties though they were more put out by the disruption of their game. Was there anything they could do to help? No, said Rodney, he'd have to cope with it himself. He turned to Miranda.

'Nice to see you back,' he said.

'I'm leaving,' she said, 'I've got a job with horses.'

So it had to be M. Ducros after all. Rodney felt almost physically sick at having misread the situation so badly. M. Ducros had a Swiss thing about keeping your house in order. What was he going to make of the reception committee? The injured womanhood brigade may have been forbidden to speak but you could bet your boots that a few of them would come up with some fairly embarrassing placards.

Rodney ran as fast as he could to his car. Nothing must go wrong on the journey. Blessedly, nothing did. He parked and ran into the terminal building.

He saw them almost at once. The main party were all together near the Nice arrival gate. The band, split into three small groups to avoid too much attention, were just preparing to converge. Mrs Milne-Thomas had her hands on the conductor's shoulders as if he were a pneumatic drill with which she was about to bore a hole in the floor. He looked helplessly at her out of his green uniform with gold facings.

Rodney glanced at the arrivals board. There it was. BE 289. Nice LANDED. Please, let there be time. He could see Mrs Barnaby marshalling the troops. He came breathlessly to her side.

'Quick,' he said, 'get everybody away. It's a false alarm. It's M. Ducros.'

She looked at him, unable to believe what he'd said. The shock of having the advantage suddenly wrested away made the urgency of withdrawal almost too much for her. She put her hands to her face.

'Quick,' Rodney repeated, 'everybody back to the bus.'

Mrs Barnaby recovered herself. 'Tell the band,' she said. The group, fortunately close knit, had got the message. They headed hastily for the stairs.

Rodney dodged his way, half running, across to Mrs Milne-Thomas and the band. She had removed her hands from the conductor's shoulders and was taking in air like an organ. The bandsmen had put on their caps and were affixing to their instruments the music for the arraignment of the Bright Seraphim.

'Make for the bus,' Rodney ordered.

There was an authority problem. They didn't know who he was.

'It's all off,' he said, keeping his voice down but motioning them desperately towards the exit. 'The bus.' The words stabbed at them. The bandsmen and Mrs Milne-Thomas started to move. Rodney turned to look towards the barrier. The Nice passengers still hadn't appeared.

At the head of the stairs he turned to look again. Still all clear. The last of the bandsmen brushed past him, cleaving a way with the extended slide of his trombone. The punitive expedition had been successfully withdrawn.

So when Barnaby arrived off the Nice plane with his new-found Finnish friend Helga Koroskinosi, a lady of seductive vowel sounds amd spectacular proportions, on whose account Miranda had left Nice two days earlier in tears, there was no one there to greet him.

6

The Caddie

Tiger had arranged a game for us at one of the smart courses near London. We were booked in with a member, Colonel Buss, one of Tiger's old comrades-in-arms. He was an eight handicap player and took his game seriously. Tiger hoped I wouldn't find him too much of a stickler. 'Give me a stickler any day of the week,' I said. 'You know where you are with a stickler.' Admittedly it isn't always where you want to be, but I didn't want to prejudice the outing.

Tiger also mentioned that he was bald with conspicuously big eyebrows. He was sensitive about that; for some reason people found it funny. I said it didn't sound that funny to me. It sounded like a slight distribution problem, but that wasn't something you laughed at.

Tiger looked at me suspiciously. 'Bald and bus jokes are absolutely out,' he said. 'Anything about two more on top and you're dead meat.'

I thanked him for the warning. It struck me that the Colonel must be a formidable customer if Tiger, who wasn't exactly timid, thought he needed handling instructions. I didn't like the sound of him.

'And I beg of you not to be late,' Tiger said. 'We're due to meet at the clubhouse at ten past nine on the whistle.'

'I'll be there,' I said.

Then I found I'd muddled up my dates and I'd be staying a good three hours' drive away. I didn't mention it to Tiger; the arrangements were all made and he was jumpy enough already that something might go wrong. There seemed no alternative but to drive down for the game and drive back afterwards; and keep quiet that I'd done it.

I apologised to my host and hostess in advance. They knew that golf was my new enthusiasm, but wasn't driving that far taking one's pleasures a little over-seriously? I explained that it was really down to Colonel Buss. If you made a plan with Colonel Buss you were expected to cross hemispheres to keep it. My host said he certainly wouldn't; you simply didn't make plans with people like that.

However I had; or, worse, Tiger had for me. They probably still thought I'd cancel once I got up there, but my mind was made up. My hostess offered to get me early breakfast before I set off. No, I said, absolutely not, nobody was to move; I'd slip out as quiet as a mouse, or, as it turned out, as quiet as a mouse that knocks a montage of Ashanti spears off the stairs wall.

I lay awake most of the night worrying about missing the alarm, allowed plenty of extra time for traffic or mishaps, and was away before dawn. Of course it was the one trip when absolutely nothing went wrong: the car engine sang, road conditions were perfect, the traffic was almost eerily quiet. I arrived ridiculously early and already tired, so I parked in a layby close to the course and revived myself with coffee out of a thermos, hoping Tiger wouldn't come by and catch me. I started the car occasionally just in case it was planning to go dead on me and I'd have to walk the last mile. It didn't and I drove up to the clubhouse at seven minutes past nine. Tiger was already there, talking to someone who was obviously Colonel Buss and another man I assumed to be Dr McGarry. They congratulated me on my precise timing.

The Colonel had mentioned that Dr McGarry would be the fourth. We gathered he was eleven handicap and had invented some sort of electronic valve that enabled him to retire from inventing and spend a lot of his time on the golf course. He lived very close to the Colonel, somewhere in the Ascot area.

I took to him at once. He spoke very quietly, with a face full of amusement. He was unassuming, benign and un-usual, a sort of human four leaf clover. He was also probably very clever, but he didn't wear his cleverness like a threat; whereas Colonel Buss was vigorously assertive, physical and galvanising, a sort of human starting handle. Just when he stood in front of me, I felt he was bombarding me with ions.

I had some small talk with Colonel Buss. Very small talk. I was careful not to look too hard at his eyebrows in case he thought I was making implicit comparisons with his bald head. As a result I must have seemed a little shifty. Tiger kept intervening on my behalf, like a mother for a small child.

'Is it the first time you've played here?' Colonel Buss asked.

'Yes, I think you said it was, didn't you?' Tiger said before I could come out with a simple yes myself.

'You'll enjoy it,' predicted Colonel Buss. 'It separates the sheep from the goats.'

That didn't sound much of a plus. I don't know which of those two creatures is worse at golf, but that's the group in which Colonel Buss evidently included me. He suggested that I should be allowed to play off the yellow tees, in deference to my status as a senior citizen. '*Droit de seigneur,*' Colonel Buss called it, which is an area where senior citizens sometimes need more than yellow tees.

A suggestion from Colonel Buss was what some of us would call an order. As it happened I was quite glad of the dispensation over the tees: some of the carries sounded quite stiff and I'm vulnerable to that, so I thanked him and he said rather flatteningly it would make a better game of it. I could see he was going to be a daunting opponent. He had a knack of diminishing you. I diminish fairly easily but Tiger didn't, and even he was in danger of turning into a ninny.

He consulted his watch, pushing back his head suddenly and raising his wrist right up so that he could squint at the time. 'Come on,' he said, rain forest eyebrows a-cluster, 'time to get cracking.'

We got cracking. The Colonel had hired caddies for everybody, 'his treat', he said, although it didn't look much of a treat to me. Mine was a veteran called Jack. He had rather a cross face as if he'd always been looking into bad weather, but he was perfectly agreeable. I didn't mind his being rather taciturn; I wasn't expecting a chat about existentialism and I certainly didn't want some sort of manic Groucho Marx making wisecracks about my game. But then I'd never really felt comfortable about having a caddie at all – in the old days because I thought they'd laugh at my clubs and because I wasn't skilful enough to take their advice, and now because I had it fixed in my mind that it was like travelling first class when the cheaper classes weren't full. Colonel Buss, more emancipated, simply wanted to play the game he was good at in the best conditions and assumed everyone else felt the same way.

Jack offered to get my clubs out of the car. I gave him the keys and he said he'd see me on the first tee. Colonel Buss shepherded us along, then started doing some loosening up exercises. He seemed very disciplined. First he did some swings with his left arm only, and finally some sizzling full practice swings. He looked a class performer. His drive howled off the tee.

Tiger drove for our side, long but slightly off line. The four of us, with the four caddies in two pairs just behind us, strode off up the fairway. The sheep were about to be separated from the goats. I began to feel a little nervous.

I should have felt much more nervous had I known that my

bag was full of drain covers. On my way to where I was staying I had called in on my daughter in the Midlands. My clubs were in the boot of my car and, while I was indoors having tea, my grandson and a small friend had filled the bottom of the bag and the pockets with all the drain covers that served the downpipes round my daughter's house and two of her neighbours' houses as well. They were of that design that gets clogged with leaves in the autumn which you prod out with a pencil. I'd noticed the two boys were giggling when they said goodbye but hoped the joke was at the expense of my daughter rather than myself. Which to some extent it was, though not enough.

The caddie must have been surprised by the weight of my bag, but he made no comment; so I hadn't the slightest suspicion there was a problem. Indeed my morale improved considerably after I struck a very decent iron shot to put our second on the edge of the green. Dr McGarry dissipated Colonel Buss's advantage off the tee with a poorish iron and our opponents were up against it. We rolled down in two putts and that was one up to us.

At the second I more or less held my own with my drive, allowing for the *droit de seigneur* advantage of the yellow tee, Tiger and the Colonel were about level pegging with two good irons, and then Tiger and I putted out in two, leaving the others playing one more. Two up.

As we set out on the long third, I had a chance to walk with Dr McGarry and belatedly congratulated him on his electronic valve. He appeared surprised that I should know about it, and modestly dismissed it as a 'one off'. Had he any other 'one offs' in mind, I wondered. Well, yes, he said, he was working on something called a lie detector, but it wasn't what I thought it was.

I asked him what it was I thought it was.

'A machine for the detection of untruths,' he said, 'as in police work and so on?'

'And what should I be thinking it is?'

'It's a device for determining what lie you've got when you're playing a simulated round on a particular course. The computer tells you exactly where your ball has finished; my device will work out your lie and this will affect the club you're permitted to use on your next shot. You also have mats of differing texture and surface – rather like, if the Colonel isn't listening to us, floor-level wigs.'

I confessed to my ignorance about the home golf industry, so between shots he told me a little about it.

He said that part of the strategy in promoting the home golf industry was to portray getting to the course and walking round it as effort. The fact that some people might call it exercise, in a pleasant setting, and even feel rather gratified by the honest weariness that comes with sporting competition, an advertising agency trained in deception could well present a four-mile walk in the rain, lugging a bag of golf clubs, as something very close to effort, if not actually the real thing.

'Very easily,' I agreed.

'Effort', Dr McGarry explained after rifling a 2 iron up the edge of the fairway, was now a pejorative word, and it was easy to press the claims of alternatives to it. You could make out a case, therefore, that what people essentially liked about golf was hitting the ball and seeing where it went, in the context of the competition they were facing and the physical circumstances of the course. It's possible to obtain these physical circumstances, in close detail, on video film; and possible therefore to play at home. You could even play matchplay rather as people used to play chess by post – still do, perhaps – and report your progress shot by shot to your opponent.

I wondered how all this would affect the actual golf courses. Would they become redundant and be turned over to sugar beet or waste disposal?

Dr McGarry thought most courses would continue much as before, the famous ones enjoying an additional income from the international sale of course cassettes. The professional circuit would be unaffected, possibly strengthened because of the interested new audience of home participants, and there would still be club fixtures at the different levels. A lot of established players would use the home facility simply as a means of getting in more hours regardless of time of day or weather conditions, and being able to play, theoretically, on an otherwise inaccessible range of international courses; but they'd probably still have the odd conventional round at their own course. It would be the new converts who would tend to be home players only, persuaded that 'effort' was best avoided. The Japanese might even play in their sleep.

As much as anything, I liked Dr McGarry's enthusiasm. As a scientific innocent I had no idea whether he was pulling my leg. I told him I hoped his lie detector would bring him further fame and fortune. He thanked me. If it did, he said, he thought he might play golf with Colonel Buss by post.

The Colonel and Tiger meanwhile, when the game allowed it, were exchanging memories of their days with the colours, although when we went four up the Colonel's capacity for reminiscence began to falter. Dr McGarry was given a mild dressing down for a lapse of concentration that put his 2 wood almost a hundred yards out of bounds, but after that the opposition was noticeably sharper. Tiger was hitting the ball well too, full of talk and confidence, and I was holding my own. Jack the caddie, without being intrusive, gave me one or two helpful tips on the idiosyncrasies of the course. I was however increasingly concerned about him. He seemed to be toiling; I had the impression that all wasn't quite well. He looked at me once or twice a little quizzically, but said nothing about the weight of the bag. I've wondered since if he'd checked to see what it was that was so heavy about it. If he did, he obviously reckoned it was in the line of duty to carry a quota of drain covers if that's what he was being paid to do. If he didn't, he must have thought there was some sort of confidentiality involved and it wasn't the form to pry into an employer's secrets. Either way he was giving himself a bad time.

At the seventh his stride began to shorten and Tiger asked me on the quiet whether there was someone in my bag. I'm afraid I laughed it off. I said that if you carried golf bags as a profession, in the course of a career you'd expect to shoulder the odd stowaway. I somehow didn't like to ask Jack if there was anything wrong. It never occurred to me that it could be the weight, and he'd surely say if he wasn't feeling well. So I still said nothing, although he was tilting over against the weight of the bag, puffing out his cheeks and generally looking very short of oil.

Just before the turn, halfway up a short steep incline, he made an odd neighing noise and subsided suddenly on to the ground. Our opponents and their caddies were up ahead; Tiger and I ran to his aid.

'That's a heavy bag,' he said, in the voice that actors in Westerns tend to use when they've just stopped three bullets in the chest in the town saloon. It's slow and pensive and usually heralds expiry, although Jack didn't look that far gone.

'Take it easy,' I said, loosening his collar, 'take it easy.' Then I lifted the bag away from him. He had a point when he said it was heavy. I stared at it in disbelief.

Tiger's caddie slipped away to signal to the others that we had a problem. I say we, but Jack in particular. They came back to join us, just in time to see a series of drain covers come clattering out of my bag as Tiger upended it on the fairway.

Colonel Buss looked from the drain covers to the seized up caddie and back again. Rational conclusions seemed to elude him. 'For Heaven's sake,' he said.

I was seriously rattled. I felt that I was in a crisis that was determined to become a disaster, something which was going to happen simply because it would be so appalling if it did. Jack was going to be permanently struck down and Colonel Buss and the rest of them would think it was my fault; there'd be resentful relatives and crippling litigation. I could tell from the look on Colonel Buss's face that it didn't occur to him that I was the victim of a trick. I don't know if he thought I was making off with the church roof, but I could see he was having doubts about my suitability to be included in a foursome in his company and on his course. And that was nothing to what he was going to think if the pile of drain covers was topped up in the next few minutes by a dead caddie.

I looked at Jack. He was very red in the face but he didn't look to be in pain. One of the caddies knelt beside him, half propping him up while he lay back with his eyes closed, breathing heavily. 'Please live,' I begged him silently.

' 'What shall we do with him?' Colonel Buss muttered to the rest of us.

We could all see the man was being inconvenient and there was a foursome coming up behind, but I thought a little more warmth of spirit mightn't have been out of place. Dr McGarry evidently thought the same.

'Give him a minute,' the caddie who was propping him up said, 'and he'll be just fine.'

That was what I wanted to hear. There was a reassuring note of experience, too, a hint of I've seen this before, in the way that he said it, although I can't believe there was a precedent in the profession for anyone being floored by drain covers. Perhaps he was just sticking up for the side.

We'd been asked to give him a minute. It passed. Colonel Buss was getting visibly fussed about the foursome behind. He turned to Dr McGarry.

'Do you think we should let them through?' he asked.

'Yes,' said Dr McGarry, 'but I'm rather more concerned about Jack.'

Colonel Buss said something about the man being all right in another minute or two, then waved the foursome through. He looked with concern at the drain covers lying on the fairway.

'Get that junk out of the way,' he said to his caddie, 'they'll wonder what the hell we're playing at.'

As his colleague started to gather up the drain covers, the patient suddenly sat up, shook his head, apologised and pronounced himself recovered. Colonel Buss looked at us all with a told-you-so expression and deputed Dr McGarry's caddie to accompany Jack back to the clubhouse. At this Jack protested unconvincingly that he was all right to go on.

'You're not,' the Colonel said sharply. 'You've given us all a nasty shock.'

Jack looked shamefaced and apologised a second time, attributing his indisposition to too much digging in his allotment. Then he allowed himself to be escorted away.

The other caddie had by now moved the drain covers off the fairway and was looking enquiringly at Colonel Buss as to what he should do with them. The Colonel clearly wanted them dumped, but I wasn't having that. They had work to do in the Midlands. So before the Colonel could give instructions I told the caddie that I'd take charge of them. I took off my pullover, loaded the pile into it, knotted the arms together, and announced I'd carry the drain covers if someone else could take my bag. The look on the Colonel's face suggested that he considered he was being unnecessarily exposed to public ridicule and that he wished there was someone present who could twiddle a ring and make him disappear. Tiger, like the good 'un he was, said he'd carry his own bag, and his caddie could take mine.

I heaved the drain covers along for the rest of the round. They had an awkward habit of bouncing up and down in my pullover, and the weight of them stretched the sleeves. Every time it was my turn to play and I set them down beside me, they made a muffled satisfactory clank.

I've seen stranger things in books of home remedies, but I'd never have expected to find myself recommending a jerseyful of drain covers if you want to clip a few shots off your golf score. I played like a demon. Dr McGarry dubbed me 'the magic plumber'. Colonel Buss exuded dislike. We won two and one.

Jack was sitting on a bench in front of the clubhouse, waiting to signal himself all right on our return. I bought him a bottle of whisky and gave it to him with some trite remark about 'kill or cure', though I didn't seriously expect it to do either. He was so appreciative that I almost warmed to him and made the mistake of asking him about his allotment. He ran through a dispiriting litany of vegetable lore, which I had eventually to interrupt, with a smilng apology, and make my way to where Colonel Buss was waiting to say goodbye. I knew my stock, already low, had sunk to nothing. He shook hands with passable grace, thanked me for the game, then added witheringly, 'Good luck with the drains.'

'Thank you,' I said, 'and good luck with the hair.'

It was childish and it was ill-mannered; but something was called for.

'Sorry,' Tiger said, 'rather a dud.'

' "All experience is an arch to build on," ' I said; and you can't get more arch than that.

Tiger didn't know I was beginning the return leg of my extended drive, and I didn't tell him. I rang my host and hostess to say I was coming up via my daughter's. 'We'll see you when we see you,' my hostess said, with more than a grain of truth.

I decided that I should go via my daughter's for two reasons; first, to restore the plumbing defences, and secondly to administer a stiff rebuke to my grandson for bringing the caddie to the brink. The drain covers travelled up on the back seat, still clanking occasionally although they were tightly wrapped up in my pullover.

I made an assertive entry to my daughter's house and laid my concealed cargo on the kitchen table.

'Where's Michael?' I asked.

'He's gone to see his friend.'

'Is that the boy who looks like a vole who was here when I left?'

She said that she hadn't noticed particularly that he looked like a vole, but yes, he had been there when I left. There was an unsatisfactory tendency in my daughter not always to side with authority.

'Would you please tell them both that their stupid joke almost caused the death of a caddie.'

'What joke?' my daughter asked.

'This joke,' I said testily, unknotting the arms of the pullover. 'They filled up my golf bag with these.'

My daughter thought it was funny. I was sorry that her husband was at his place of work because he might have brought a note of realism into the conversation. I suspected, too, that the boys might have been more wary of removing the drain covers had he been there to supervise.

I stayed for tea, trying to conserve my indignation, but Michael didn't return. I think my daughter had telephoned the vole's mother to tell her to hang on to them both until I'd gone. Discipline seemed to have gone to the wall.

'I'm sorry to have missed Michael and his friend the vole,' I said, standing up to leave, 'but at least you're reunited with your plumbing.'

As a corrective mission it was something of a failure. I wondered, as I set off on the final lap, what I should have said had Jack expired. For that matter, I wondered what Mrs Jack or the fellow allotment-tenders would have said had

Jack expired. Happily, it was a sterile exercise. I cleared my mind of drain covers and concentrated on the unfolding road.

When I got in, my host and hostess had just finished rearranging the montage of Ashanti spears, which I'd left in a pile on a hall chair with a note of apology on the top. The mishap seemed nicely to symbolise our colonial collapse, although my host and hostess may have seen it simply as an act of clumsiness.

'A long day,' my host said. 'How did it go?'

I decided only on the broader picture. 'We won two and one,' I said.

7
Legal Eagle

It was always said that the case of Christabel Tetley was a high point in Humphrey Overton's career at the bar. He would have agreed with that. Shortly afterwards he was appointed a Queen's Bench judge. Shortly after that, in an escalation of good fortune, he found himself playing a single against me at Brancaster on the north Norfolk coast and being rather impertinently quizzed about his professional attitudes.

The Tetley case had attracted wide interest in the golfing world, where Overton's understanding of the game was thought by many to have been crucial in seeing his client through. What had impressed the golfers was the way he titillated the jury over the respective lethal potentials of a sand iron and a 3 iron.

Yes, but wait a minute. The point he was making was that if you're going to murder someone you would always choose to hit them with the sand iron and not the number 3. That particular familiarity with the clubs may give you a few extra stars as a murderer but I don't think it makes any appreciable difference to the standard of your golf. If you're relying on these murder weapons in terms, for instance, of how best to stop your ball on the twelfth green at Brancaster, you may find it irrelevant that you know roughly how much damage the different irons will cause if brought down hard on a human skull.

There were aspects of the Tetley case which were distinctly odd, and it was no surprise that it caught the public imagination at the time. Maurice Tetley, Christabel's husband, according to those who knew him at the Midland golf club where he was a member, was a mild-mannered, rather likeable man who played off a twelve handicap, though the handicap was hardly a factor in the brief contest with Christabel when she clubbed him to death with a 3 iron. She didn't deny that she had caused his death, but she pleaded self-defence.

It depended on Humphrey Overton therefore to convince the jury that the impression created by Maurice at the golf club was not a true reflection of his character; that he was in fact a domestic ogre, given to outbursts of unreasonable behaviour. There were few better than Overton QC at nosing out these unsuspected anomalies. He knew what every susceptible juryman and woman knows – that, if you've the will, you can find a potential Bluebeard in every suburban two up, two down, and a serial killer waiting for the call in every convent. It's just a question of pointing up the quirky moments into symptoms of criminal tendency. What was anyone's guess was quite why Christabel Tetley chose to stay around if her husband really was what Overton made him out to be. Certainly it was one of the questions posed by the prosecution which should have received more sympathetic attention from the jury. But the jury didn't get to considering inconvenient truths when Overton QC was in full swing. The witnesses came and went, Overton roasted and poached them in sequence, until the seemingly amicable characteristics of the victim were being accepted as yet one more proof of the old saw that you can't tell a sausage by its skin – particularly when it's been roughed up with a 3 iron.

'The first club that came to hand. . .'

All this was the familiar staple of courtroom drama. But Overton at a late stage of the proceedings established two further crucial pieces of so-called evidence – that both he and his client were themselves passably experienced golfers and that no one choosing to kill his or her spouse would take a 3 iron with which to do it. A sand iron, Overton explained – and demonstrated – to the court, would certainly have been the golfer's choice.

At this moment we freeze the frame. What has this to do with golfing skills? Nothing much. The golfer will reasonably predict, just as anyone considering using an offensive weapon will reasonably predict, which lump of metal will best serve his or her purpose. But it highlights Overton at work. He makes out that as we are discussing golfing equipment, albeit used in a non-golfing context, the golfers' expertise is implicit in anything to do with the handling of it. The jury, thick good men and true, believe this.

Overton could then progress to explain to the jury that if Christabel had wielded a 3 iron it was evident that as a golfer, since no caddy was involved, she had snatched the first club that came to hand and was clearly defending herself from attack by the victim. The judge was rightly sceptical about Overton's somewhat theatrical explanation, but the jury, who were awake at this point almost to a man, thought it a convincing and accessible argument. Judge uneasy; Christabel walks free.

The case had greatly intrigued me. In pulling off this defence Overton himself acquired a wholly unfounded reputation as a golfer. Conversely, and most important, all of us now knew that when we had the choice of using either a 3 iron or a sand iron and we chose the 3 iron, however disastrous the result, we were establishing that we couldn't be murderers. This was the Overton exoneration theory; and it was extremely mischievous.

Then, by an extraordinary chance, I came into personal

contact with Overton. I was one of Uncle Reggie's executors, concerned with the sale after his death of the house in Norfolk. Who should appear as a potential buyer but the celebrated Humphrey Overton, now a High Court judge. There was something quietly comic about anything to do with Uncle Reggie passing to a prominent member of the legal establishment, and it was a fitting facet of this last Uncle Reggie joke that he should miss it by being dead.

Helen and I were staying at Pitremington Hall, supervising the changeover. The last of Uncle Reggie's paying guests had been carted off to pay elsewhere and we were explaining to Humphrey Overton and his wife how everything worked at the Hall – not an arduous task because not much did. I happened to mention, being familiar with Overton's golfing connection, that I had taken up the game. He perked up at this and we arranged to have a round together at Brancaster before Helen and I set off back to Dorset.

I don't think I expected to quiz Overton directly about the Tetley case, but I was interested to talk to him. I should have liked to have heard his own opinion on the validity of the defence – beyond the fact, and quite an important one, that it came off – and to find out whether to him this was just another job, from which he kept his private emotions distanced, or whether his own aptitude for golf had given it a special colour.

The Royal West Norfolk club's links at Brancaster adorn a wonderful remote stretch of coast, eyed menacingly by the sea. During spring tides the marsh adjoining the course can flood and defences seem precarious should there be a major storm. Beyond the dunes, when the wind is up, you hear the ceaseless rumble of the waves along the shore line. The sailing's good and the bird life exceptional, attended regularly by bands of twitchers brought in from far and wide by news of an unexpected sighting.

The judge and I agreed on a sedate single. The first drive is over a chasm and I was so apprehensive as to what a topped drive would do for my morale that I played slow and safe, with the result that I had far too much to do on the second shot, which is supposed to find the green up towards your left. After three holes I was three down.

The fourth is short but full of trouble. It's 128 yards from the high tee to the flag on the high plateau green, perched over a bank revetted with sleepers. I managed to lodge on the green after the judge caught the top of the bank and rolled back into a bunker designed to penalise exactly that shot.

I risked it. 'Looks like you'll need the murder weapon.'

'Ah,' he said, 'do I see smoke signals of the Tetley case?'

'Do you mind?'

'Not really,' he replied, 'I'm quite used to it. I don't think it was my best moment but, as it turned out, it was certainly a good one for Christabel Tetley. You could call it advocate's flourish.'

'As taught at the Errol Flynn school of swordsmanship?'

He laughed. 'Not completely dissimilar, though we don't swing in on the chandeliers.'

I'd made my breakthrough. He talked freely and most interestingly about the ethics of advocacy, as we played along the seaward side of the links, before turning for the second half.

At the twelfth we were confronted with our test case. He had a simple choice to use a sand iron and take the lofted line to the green or to use a 3 iron and take the low road. In the courtroom, on behalf of Christabel Tetley, he had suggested that it was inconceivable that anyone planning to murder who knew about golf would have chosen the 3 in preference to the sand iron. Now it seemed that if you wanted to do something more complicated with your golf clubs, like play golf shots, instead of smashing in your spouse's head, club selection was a much more difficult business. This seemed to be telling me something about golf and something about the law; and I wasn't certain that I wanted to know either.

The judge was really in a quandary, holding a club in each hand, but quite without the authority he had shown towards the jury at the Tetley trial.

'A teaser, m'lud?' I enquired.

I could see he was not only battling with indecision but he was conscious of looking indecisive.

'The problem is,' he said, 'whether I can stop the 3 iron on this moonscape.'

'Then go for the murderer's friend.'

'I'll take the 3 iron,' he said. The shot ran too fast across the green and ran on to the fairway behind.

'Wrong choice,' he said.

'Tell that to Maurice Tetley,' I said.

We sat together after the round looking out over the shore and dunes, listening to the seabirds. It's the wildness that paradoxically gives the place its calm.

The judge was an agreeable fellow. He loved Brancaster, he said; he'd played holiday golf there for as long as he could remember. It would be too awful if it was surrendered to the sea, while all the interested parties were agreeing that something had to be done but hoping individually they weren't going to have to pay. The old Brancaster connection was really why he'd bought Uncle Reggie's house. Not that the part of Norfolk around Pitremington was anything like Brancaster, so it seemed a tenuous connection. But then, he went on, 'You've still got the skies and the wonderful light. When you talk about that, people always say "Oh everybody says that" in a dismissive way. As if because everybody says something it becomes untrue.'

Nevertheless, I told him I thought he was a brave man acquiring a house that had belonged to Uncle Reggie.

'In what way?' he asked.

'I'm not competent to assess what happens after death,' I said, 'but I can't believe St Peter's going to be that thrilled to see Uncle Reggie forming up at the gates. He's sure to have lost his documentation , and they'll put him into spooking.'

'You think they'll give him his old home patch?'

'I don't think Uncle Reggie's spooking would be graced by any sort of planning. Not by the authorities anyway .'

'Do you think we should lock up our sand irons at night?'

'I don't see Uncle Reggie as a killer. Funnily enough, he was always a sort of human poltergeist. He emanated rogue energy all his life. No, I think he'll just break everything and not replace it. Business as usual, really.'

'I'm sorry you didn't mention this when we were completing the purchase.'

I felt like Eric and Deric with their 'spot of the old caveat emptor'.

'Come on,' I said. 'As lived in by Uncle Reggie? Worth double.'

8

They're Playing Our Shot

It was a shot with a 6 iron that had won Bradley Butterfield the hand of his wife Betty, not to mention the rest of her. The River Wharfe runs alongside the first seven holes at Ilkley and Bradley had played with one foot in the water and run the ball up to within six inches of the pin. 'Watch this,' he'd called ahead; and to the admiring Betty it encapsulated his winning ways. The recollection of that shot ran through their married life with a sentimental identity of its own. So when Bradley, in his cups, asked me to reenact it for his wife when we three played at Ilkley, I could hardly say no; though for me nothing hung on the shot – I was rather beyond the days of courting and not much stirred by Betty Butterfield's attractions.

She was ten years younger than I, but I'd known her since childhood. Her doctor father, Arthur Johnson, had been my father's partner, both of them Yorkshiremen by birth who for some reason had found their way down to Hampshire. Betty's grandfather was a doctor too, mine a clergyman-ornithologist from the old North Riding. That's why I'd been sent to a boarding school at the top of the dales and learnt my wet fly fishing on the upper reaches of the Wharfe – the same Wharfe that punishes, and sometimes confiscates, the Ilkley golfers' wayward shots.

Arthur Johnson's wife I remember well. She was forthright Yorkshire under a veneer of refinement. Her family had done nicely in construction. She had a very definitive enunciation – my father used to laugh at the way she often said 'Likewise', endorsing some order or opinion. The syllables came out exactly like her bosom, both parts rounded and of even emphasis, with just the briefest intermission in between. Betty was the Johnsons' only child and I'm sure it was a happiness to Mrs Johnson in particular that the Yorkshire connection was restored when Betty got engaged to Bradley Butterfield on Ilkley golf course.

Over the years she'd broadened out, and her centre of gravity had descended to a point that would have made her almost impossible to blow over in the strongest wind. She had a cheery face like an apple, a formidable appetite, and her hair, full and grey, rode up and down as if on springs. Her head was screwed on in good Yorkshire fashion, but if anything a little too tight – at the expense of the length of her neck. For all that, she'd been a useful singer in her day, although the pitch of her voice was deeper than you'd expect. Perhaps it was something to do with the shortness of her neck, the sound may have escaped too soon. Bradley used to say he didn't know if his wife was 'a ballless baritone or a mezzanine'. But let Betty loose on something like 'Blow the Wind Southerly' and she'd sing the pattern off your plates. She was colossal. She was the diva of the dales.

The Butterfields were also in construction, and young Bradley was distinctly 'warm' from the profits of Butterfield Homes. After he and Betty were married they lived in a solid house on the edge of Ilkley, which wasn't quite pretentious but far from self-effacing; and certainly not a Butterfield Home. There was a rockery in the garden which Bradley built himself and adorned with miniature windmills which yodelled as the sails blew round. The back lawn was converted into a putting course with small red flags and a grass surface so smooth that you'd have thought it was ironed. Betty once did five holes in one on the trot and was rewarded by Bradley with a big silver cup which stood in the dining room, inscribed – above the date – BETTY BUTTERFIELD – ILKLEY'S PUTTING QUEEN.

They were a port of call if ever we went north that way – Bradley and Betty I'm afraid referred to their house as our 'Ilkley B & B', and perhaps for us convenience came into it as much as obligation. Besides, Betty was part of the folklore of my younger days and there was a welcoming awfulness about Bradley that you couldn't dislike. There was always a friendly atmosphere about the house, principally because Bradley and Betty were very pleased with each other and doted on their daughter Iona. She was known at home as 'Princess' and at the golf club as 'Iona chunk of Ilkley'. She was well turned out and a little earnest; if you were unlucky enough to get trapped she'd tell you about the other students on her economics course. I could see her marrying into construction; she was a consolidator, not a pioneer. But that was the family tradition.

Bradley was very handy about the house and was constantly showing me little tricks of repair and embellishment – the repair usually technically beyond me, the embellishment nearly always contrary to my taste. He was also mad about gadgets; the kitchen was full of them and he was constantly whirring them into action while he kept up a shouted commentary about where he'd got them and the edge they seemed to have over everyone else's models. It was all rather confusing; I was always nervous someone might end up as a puree if they stood in the wrong place.

What was hard to take about Bradley's zest for instruction was that he seemed more concerned with parading his experience than with any help it might be to someone else. As it happened, his hints, particularly about golf, could be quite useful if you could bring yourself to listen to them. Experience can usually save inexperience the odd shot; and everyone likes saving the odd shot – even at the price of being exposed to Bradley Butterfield's instruction. But as far as I was concerned, Bradley had always been a reason I'd been glad that I wasn't a golfer; and now that I was, I knew what to expect.

To start with, there was this sickly story of their betrothal. I'd heard it loads of times before of course; Betty used to simmer at the sheer romance of it – 'Just you show me you can do it, Bradley Butterfield' and sure enough he struck it dead, with the mayor's sister looking on. 'How's that for starters, Betty Johnson?' It was the ultimate 'gimme'. And give him she did.

They threw an engagement party in the clubhouse. In due course Bradley rose to become the captain and Betty won the Ladies' Medal three times in nine years. Not many of the members escaped without a tip or two on the importance of posture or some dos and don'ts that Bradley had accumulated about playing out of wet sand. The Princess, who had no chance of evading the effusion of advice, must have been the most highly instructed junior in the North. She planed down her handicap with a beautifully rhythmic swing; her golfing etiquette was impeccable; to her parents she was wish-fulfilment. She was Julie Andrews in plus fours.

Now I'd taken up golf and I was going north, on my own. I radioed on ahead, as it were, announcing my conversion.

Bradley answered the telephone. He gave a disbelieving whoop. 'D'you hear that Betty?' he called (though as she sounded to be in another room, I couldn't think that she had), 'he's taken up golf.'

'Who has?' I heard her ask. He told her. The whoop this time was in Betty's throaty 'mezzanine'. 'Taken up golf? I don't believe it.'

'It's true,' Bradley assured her, 'he's just told me himself.'

They wanted to hear every detail – where, why, when. I

'Ilkley's Putting Queen'

tried to tell them I'd be stopping with them for two days, if that was possible, and I'd give them all the news then.

'We'll all have a round together,' Bradley said. 'I'm sure I can give you a few tips.'

'I'm sure you can.' I was sure he would.

'Practice, old boy,' Bradley said. 'It's all down to practice.'

'So they tell me,' I said.

'You know what Gary Player said: "The more I practise, the luckier I get." '

'Very witty.'

'Very wise too,' Bradley said.

Yes, I agreed, it was both very witty and very wise.

'I've got lots more like that,' Bradley promised.

'I'll look forward to them,' I said.

I like Ilkley. It's dressed as a hydro, and it still has a sort of propriety, a feeling of deposit account brass. I don't go much on the moor, but that's entirely because of that dreadful song. I see it as a sort of topographical attic, an attraction you don't actually have to toil up to see, and I hope all those good hotels and houses realise that being nearer the top is only an advantage because the view downhill's much better. And that, for most of the town, takes in the golf course, sensibly spread beyond the through road and the river to give the place some leisurely rich breadth. I don't know how many people have got engaged there – probably not so many as have decided to get divorced – but Bradley and Betty did. He always gave her a special look on that green as he holed out and she responded in a private sort of way. It says a lot for their marriage that they played hundreds and hundreds of rounds there; I think they regarded a game at Moortown or Pannal as adultery.

I arrived, by a quirk of faulty timing, just in time for tea.

'Still got the old car then,' Bradley said, banging the bonnet with the flat of his hand. 'Elastic still holding up?'

'Good as new,' I said.

'Well, come on in. Betty's got us a cracking tea.'

I didn't like the sound of that. There was something of the taxidermist about Betty when it came to catering. I followed Bradley into the house carrying a box of golf balls I'd brought them as a present.

'Betty!' I had to exclaim when I saw the tea table. 'Who's coming to tea? Leeds?'

'I bought some of your favourites,' Betty said. 'Specially. We don't see you very often.'

'You'll never see me at all', I replied, 'if I eat all this lot.'

'Tea'll never hurt you. You're scraggy,' Bradley said, putting two fishpaste sandwiches into his mouth. It was both a compliment and a personal remark.

'Bradley,' Betty said, 'don't jump the gun.'

I fumbled with my present. 'A little gift,' I said, 'between golfers.'

I gave it to Betty. Bradley peered over as she started to unwrap it. 'Give us a roll of drums,' he said. 'It's the Crown Jewels.'

'I'm afraid not,' I had to admit, 'it's a box of golf balls.'

'Same thing,' Bradley said, wresting it away from Betty and approving the make. 'Do you know about these balls?' he asked. 'Do you know how many leading professionals played with these in the last Open?'

Of course I didn't know, and had I done so it would have spoiled what he was going to tell me anyway. But at least I'd apparently chosen the right brand. I stood there pretending to listen as he told me about their special properties. Betty seemed to be preoccupied with an inventory of the tea table.

'Amazing story, isn't it?' he said, indicating that his recounting of the story was complete.

'You wouldn't have thought there was so much involved in making a golf ball,' I said, hoping this would complement what he'd been telling me. He looked at me rather oddly, so I suspect it didn't.

Bradley said he'd show me up to my room. There was a pile of golf books by the bed. He started picking them up as I was unpacking my suitcase, and reading bits out to me. I said I'd look forward to going through them, although I couldn't be sure I'd be doing anything after going the full distance with Betty's tea.

It was certainly a challenge. My two conflicting priorities, of not hurting Betty's feelings and of not exploding, fought for supremacy. Betty began to give a conducted tour of the attractions.

'French fancies, pikelets, Battenbergs, Garibaldis, special Skipton meringues ...'

'Betty,' I said. 'It's a feast. I'll blow up.'

'Oh come on,' she said, 'you know what they say; a little of what you fancy does you good.'

'No,' I said, 'what they say is: a *little* of what you fancy does you good.'

The two of them looked at me incredulously.

'Well, shovel my Aunt Fanny through a glass darkly,' Bradley said, lowering to his plate the section of uneaten meringue that wasn't affixed to his cheek.

'People who talk in epigrams about our moral condition,' I said loftily, 'tend to be advocates of restraint.'

'Say again,' said Bradley.

'It's the wet blanket principle,' I explained.

I got off fairly lightly over the tea. Betty did look a little disappointed, I have to admit. My conscience advised a dozen or so more favourites, but my stomach said no. I excused myself and said I'd have a short rest after the day's driving, if that was all right, and see them later.

'Dinner's at eight,' Betty said. 'It's going to be a bit special,' Bradley added.

It was more than that. It was a cavalcade, with a range of superfluous delights to which, Betty explained, she and Bradley couldn't say no.

The conversation centred principally on a dissection of my brief golfing career. Bradley turned this threadbare topic into a cross-examination about my mini-professional's teaching techniques and my performance on individual courses. As he'd played on only one of them, he had very little to which to relate; but he kept up a barrage of enquiries. The two of them, meanwhile, plied me constantly with food and drink. I felt wedged into my chair and more than slightly inebriated. When Bradley suggested that the two of us adjourn to the golf room, I found I had lost the power of organised resistance and heard myself saying 'I'd love to.'

The golf room was an extension of the garage. It was about twice the size of a squash court and committed to the serious business of practice. I can't remember how many chip shots I hit into the armchair or how many putts grazed along the skirting board as I stood with my head touching the wall. Bradley said this was useful because it eliminated any tendency to sway – something that couldn't be claimed for Betty's dinners. I hit shots with my legs together, I hit shots into a net, I hit one shot that went through a small hole near the top of the net and sang round the room with a velocity that would have killed us. Then there was a protracted routine of tapping a car tyre that was some fad of Henry Cotton's. Bradley gripped me, steered me, bent me. At his injunction I forgot the right arm, maintained the triangle. I just wonder whether all the tips were filtering through to the improvement of my game.

Every now and then he sploshed some more red wine into his glass. I'd called a halt by now. I thought he was building up to something, and he was. Quite unembarrassed, he asked whether, when we played with Betty in the morning, I could contrive to re-enact the famous betrothal shot.

'I'll try, of course,' I said, taken aback. 'But I'm sure to make a hash of it.'

'Doesn't matter,' he said. 'I didn't.'

There was a large poster on the wall. Bradley had had it copied from one at John Jacobs's golf range at Sandown Park. It read:

First understand what it is you are trying to do. The only purpose of the golf swing is to move the club through the ball square to the target at maximum speed. How this is done is of no significance at all so long as the method employed is to be done repetitively.

Bradley said he'd take me through it. He put an empty wine bottle on the floor and began to intone the unimpeachable good sense of the poster. But by then I had absolutely no idea what I was trying to do, except – instinctively – escape to bed. The phrases began to belabour me into non-comprehension.

He switched me on to bunker shots. I can hear his voice now, in a slow, heavy rhythm, like some plastered choirmaster, 'Smoothly along your shoulder line ... Down and through ... Out to in ... Pick and chop ... Hands *ahead* of the clubface.'

Finally I fell face forward onto the armchair into which I'd pitched, throughout the evening, at least a hundred balls.

'No, Bradley, no,' I begged him. 'I can't go on.'

There was silence. Ashamed, I pulled myself back out of the chair and turned to face him. He was still moving his head from side to side as if to the rhythm of the phrases. He laid an arm round my shoulder and leant heavily against me.

'I hope it's been useful,' he said in a slurred voice.

'Yes,' I said gently, 'I'm sure it has.'

I eased out from under his arm to go off to bed. He fell on the floor and I left him there.

I wasn't aware when I woke up that my after-dinner session with Bradley had dramatically improved my game. If any good had come of it, it was perhaps the tip about putting with your head against the wall. It's not an option that's available to you in match play, unless something very curious has happened, but it does bring home to you how much more consistent you are if you keep your head steady. It's obviously something you have to do for yourself, but at least you've had practical confirmation that it makes a difference. For that very good reason it creates confidence; and without that you're lost on the green.

In this connection I'm also sure that the simple trick of imagining that you're aiming at a six-foot circle – of which the hole happens to be the centre – stands you in good stead. It gets back to confidence again: hitting the ball into a six-foot circle seems easy, whereas hitting it into that little hole certainly doesn't. The result is that you're nearly always close, and occasionally you're better than that.

Instruction books on golf all seem to be in favour of warming up before a game. At my level of golf I don't see myself keeping everyone waiting while I fire off scores of different shots on the practice course. But I do a few basic exercises before the off, like swinging with two clubs quite slowly. At my age, and without the lifetime's discipline of a Gary Player, anything too dramatic could be self-defeating: I don't want to seize up before the game actually gets under way, so I don't favour the Cossack dancer routine on the first tee or rabbit jumps over the sand box. Besides, everyone longs for you to do an airshot if you display yourself as a gymnastic machine. So I just get what blood there is moving round the system, and leave techniques like the 'Williams' to people who like impersonating hedgehogs.

Bradley and I had a short session in the golf room before setting out for the course – which was only a few minutes from the house. I hoped he wouldn't remember raising the subject of the betrothal shot, but he mentioned it again.

'For old times' sake,' he said.

I could hardly refuse, though the role of Cupid isn't one that sits easily on me.

The course is well looked after, pretty flat, and if you can avoid the obvious hazards like the River Wharfe, not too challenging for the steady player. Bradley and Betty could have played it blindfold. They gave nothing away; their line was unerring, there was a discipline about their golf and a harmony about their partnership which was a pleasure to see. Bradley, predictably, kept up a barrage of hints, some-times – as my line was more wayward – delivered from quite a distance. I didn't consciously take any notice of any of them, but when a shot went well he thought I had and became a little proprietorial about my success. Betty, trundling along with her low centre of gravity and her socks turned down over her ankles, left the vocals to her husband. There was something very thorough about her progress up the course; you half expected straight wide stripes to emerge behind her on the grass. Bradley made no attempt to instruct her, there was a solidity about their partnership that had transferred to life; or perhaps, given the betrothal shot, it was the other way round.

When we came to the point of the embarrassing reenactment I deliberately muffed my second right to the edge of the river, adjusting it with a surreptitious kick to more or less the position from which Bradley had hit the betrothal shot. They were walking on together towards the green and I saw Bradley pointing out to Betty that I was playing their shot. She took his arm. I guessed that there was a romantic frisson merely in my addressing of the ball in this position. A rhythmic chorus of Bradley's tips began to throb in my head as I settled to the shot with one foot balanced on a stone at the edge of the river. Slowly back, and a great conviction overtook me as if a massive outbreak of violins would burst from the amphitheatre of the town behind me. Sweet was the strike and true the flight; right on to the dance floor and terribly, terribly close to the band. A hundred and thirty yards away my triumph stirred my opponents into a passionate embrace that was nostalgia dressed as lust.

If I had turned the key I was not interested in opening the door. Bradley stood with his arm around Betty's shoulders as I walked up towards the green.

'That's my lad,' he shouted, raising his putter above his head. Then he did a lunging, aerial kick of triumph and with a howl of sudden pain fell on his back, locked in a muscular spasm and quite unable to move.

Four of us brought him back to the clubhouse on a gate. One at each corner, with Betty walking alongside holding his hand. His face was working with something that I hope was closer to frustration than pain. It taught me something about nostalgia. I hope it taught him.

9

The McTeak

Tiger and I had gone north. It wasn't quite the same as my annual fishing expeditions, but it was still Scotland and if you're converted to golf this has to be one of your pilgrimages. The plan was to play at Prestwick and, to get really reverential, at St Andrews, interspersed with less heady competition at a little course near where we were staying, where our elderly Scottish host was club president and owned the land. He was called The McTeak, not because of his intellect, as some unkindly said, but because he was the top McTeak, the peak McTeak, and adopted the definitive 'The,' as Scots do, to clarify his station. Something quite serious seemed to have happened to the rest of the clan, because they scarcely got a mention in the telephone directory that covered their traditional stamping ground; so either they didn't like keeping in touch or they hadn't been kindly treated by the passing of time.

We – that is Helen and myself and Tiger and Mrs Tiger – were installed with the old gentleman. He told me almost as soon as we arrived he'd been Tiger's godfather. I knew that; it was how Tiger had explained him. I don't know on what basis Tiger's parents had selected godparents for their son, but I suspect that mastery of the scriptures bulked a poor second to owning some decent fishing – if it was in the placings at all.

The house was substantial rather than comfortable. It had been redefended against the cold in the 1920s, but not very successfully and I shouldn't have liked to have experienced it in the depths of winter. Helen and I had a huge bathroom that had been adjusted from being a bedroom by substituting a towel horse and a wooden chair for all the furniture and siting a small claw-footed bath under the window. The noise of the hot water pipes in the morning as the guests began to stir was like the opening of the Anvil Chorus. It signalled the progress towards the bathrooms of a limited quantity of peaty brown water that was at first quite dangerously hot but soon dried up altogether with some dying coughs of scale from the mouth of the tap.

The architecture was austere, giving the weather back as good as it got, with turrets on the corners and a fine view over open country, quite a bit of which The McTeak still owned, although the estate had diminished considerably during the period of his stewardship. He was proud of the length of his lineage, but without much inspiration as to how it might be perpetuated in any sort of style. A rather bad-tempered housekeeper presided over the domestic arrangements. There had been a Mrs McTeak, a grim-faced woman to judge from her photographs (unless the photographs had themselves caught sight of the dreadful portrait of her in the hall); but she'd been carried off by illness, leaving The McTeak in his declining years rather at the mercy of the housekeeper, and mercy, to judge from our brief acquaintance, came from that direction in fairly short supply.

There is a sort of sidelined interest about such people, and I was curious to know why our host seemed to have been marooned in isolation from his clan. Why this mysterious diaspora of the McTeaks? Had they all taken off for the New World; or had there been some demographic blip that had resited them in areas more likely to provide them some employment? I all but learnt the secret on our very first evening. We were sitting by the fire after dinner – well, it wasn't exactly a fire, more an asphyxiating exercise in drying out extremely wet wood – when The McTeak asked me if I'd like to hear the history of the clan. If you call yourself The McTeak you must reckon that the answer to that question is yes, and as far as I was concerned, indeed it was. I cantered my chair eagerly towards him but for some reason he looked distracted and started talking to Mrs Tiger about airedales. So for the moment the McTeak diaspora remained a riddle.

He'd obviously been a keen golfer in his day. Apart from the little course nearby, where they couldn't keep him out as he was effectively the proprietor, he told us more than once that he was a member of five of Scotland's best-known clubs. He told us less than once (though somebody else filled in for him) that in fact he'd been a member of six but had resigned from one of them in rather embarrassing circumstances.

What had happened was this. He was a tireless upholder of club rules, believing rigidly in traditional standards of dress and behaviour that the rules had been orginally drafted to accommodate. One day, in a particularly cantankerous moment, he complained to the secretary that someone purporting to be a gentleman had come into the dining room wearing a silk neckerchief (as he preposterously called it) instead of a tie. This was in breach of club rules. The man must be slung out of the dining room.

The secretary looked extremely hunted at this directive, because The Neckerchief enjoyed quite as much status as The McTeak and infinitely more popularity. The secretary mc-ummed and mc-aahed; The McTeak ordered him to stop doing both those things and to discharge the duties for which he was handsomely paid.

Tartan with embarrassment, the secretary did as he was

told and asked to have a private word with The Neckerchief. The Neckerchief, in some surprise, came to the secretary's office and was told that a member in the dining room was insisting on strict interpretation of the rules – which, well, meant no lunch for Neckerchiefs.

The Neckerchief understood the secretary's dilemma and behaved quite restrainedly towards him. He did ask, however, if the secretary would let him know the identity of the member who'd lodged the complaint. The secretary said he was very sorry, but that was something he couldn't possibly do. In that case, The Neckerchief said, he would conduct his own enquiries; and he stormed into the dining room, where in a very loud voice he called for the idiot who'd been complaining about his dress to stand up.

Nobody got to their feet. The Neckerchief repeated his question, adding, persuasively, that *somebody* in the room must have done it and nobody's memory could be that bad.

At this The McTeak informed The Neckerchief that it was he who had quite properly complained and instead of throwing his weight about in this boorish way he might spend a few constructive moments memorising the club rules.

The Neckerchief, slightly taken aback by this evenly delivered rebuke, suggested that no sensible club could rule his dress out of order.

The McTeak said he was a member of six first-class golf clubs and he should know about such things.

'If you're a member of six first-class golf clubs,' The Neckerchief replied, 'I suggest you —— well spend a lot more time at the other five.'

At this a ripple of applause ran through the dining room, then swelled significantly in volume. And The McTeak there and then resigned.

He said he wouldn't come with us to Prestwick, which was just as well as Tiger and I had fixed up with two old fishing friends of mine, one of whom was a member there. It's really the scene of the crime: the first Open Championship was held at Prestwick in 1860. It's the same old challenge, with the dunes and the coarse rough, a respected enemy if you're beating it, and something unprintable if you're not. I'm not sure I want to know that in 1870 young Tom Morris holed the (then) 578-yard first in three and went round thirty-six holes in 149, with clubs that make mine look the ultimate in sophistication, and putting on greens that were mown with a scythe. That sort of thing cuts you down to size, and not very large size at that.

The only inside information I had about the club, and as it came from The McTeak it might not have been blue chip, was that they drank more kummel there than at any other golf course. The McTeak's knowledge of the course didn't extend to the playing surfaces, but he'd picked up this statistical snippet on his travels. I don't know whether they'd chosen kummel because it was a record the other clubs wouldn't try to take off them, or because it was a necessary protection from the prevailing wind. Tiger thought it was to do with the wind, but illogically drank his three glasses after we'd finished our round and were safely in the shelter of the clubhouse.

We were playing a foursome – Tiger and I against my two old fishing friends. Both of them were pretty competent and, looking at the course, I was afraid that their local knowledge might be a significant advantage. The wind, which hadn't seemed too bothersome when we were setting off, began to bully us, and in those circumstances all the conspiracies against a decent score begin to pull together – the greens seem to get smaller, the normal terrain degenerates into endless bumps and hollows, there's always a bunker to catch the very last roll of your ball. My spirits began to sag. My performance at the third was typical. It's called the Cardinal, and it has a huge sleepered bunker into which I duly hit our second like a man in a trance. The worst thing about it was that I knew I was going to do it; I told the others I was going to do it; and then I did it. It was exactly according to plan, except the plan somehow wasn't mine.

The fifteenth has a fairway like a wasp waist and a tiny green awaiting the shot that doesn't find a bunker; and in this unlikely setting I suddenly hit a vein of freak good form, which lasted until I holed a long one on the eighteenth green and went into the clubhouse in a mood of unexpected elation. But on balance I felt about Prestwick, in the wind, as Rossini felt about Wagner – lovely moments but awful quarters of an hour.

So what of St Andrews? Standing on the first, addressing my tee shot, I felt like a rude boy in a cathedral, unable to shout some terrible word because he believes the place actually has powers of retribution. Now that I'm out of its way, I can admit that it didn't come up to my expectations. But, rather like the Rowley mile course at Newmarket, it's passable if you like your vistas bleak and it's great if you feel the presence of ghosts.

Our round – no, it wasn't a round, it was nine holes that took an eternity – was blighted, I'm sorry to say, by the company. That sounds ungrateful, but it's intended merely to be factual. The McTeak had set up the visit for us, and made us feel we were very lucky – he was playing godfather again, giving us a treat. And that involved a friend of his who was apparently a big wheel in the golfing world. As Tiger said to me afterwards, he may have been a big wheel but he went round incredibly slowly. Had I been playing behind us, and had I not been pathologically timid, I think I would have loosed off a prompter towards his backside. I suppose he was an accepted 'character', and any complaining letters to the secretary would have been considered out of turn; but he wasn't a happy combination with The McTeak.

On his own course The McTeak was even worse. We hadn't been under way very long when I began to get intimations of serious trouble. The McTeak's style of play was exasperating. He would change his mind several times about his choice of club and spend ages staring in the direction of the green. The caddie evidently knew his man, just as he knew it was more than his job was worth to say what must have been on his mind. But no such inhibitions affected the fourball behind us.

They were holidaymakers, three of them from the North Country, the other a Scot. Everything about their demeanour and appearance made me wish that some malicious fate hadn't directed them to the first tee immediately after us. Two were wearing T-shirts with rather racy slogans, and one braces and distinctly overstated tartan plus fours. They were noisy, cheerful and not at all susceptible to any show of authority that might hamper their holday enjoyment. Their golf was similarly forceful.

It soon became apparent that they thought our progress much too slow. There were shouts of 'Get a shift on, Methuselah,' when The McTeak was agonising over whether to take a 5 or a 6 iron. He didn't respond to this discourteous intervention, possibly because it didn't occur to him that anyone would be addressing him in such a way. But the rest of us heard it; and we had no doubt that there was more – and worse – to come.

Next they started barracking his shots. They cheered when he struck an indifferent iron shot at the third and he looked round in considerable surprise to see where the noise was coming from. He waved his iron at them quite good-humouredly and they whistled and gesticulated back.

It was when The McTeak stopped the round to point out to us some geographical feature that the men behind us stepped up their campaign of criticism. One of them played earlier than golfing etiquette would normally permit, with the result that the ball overtook The McTeak – not full toss but definitely at a speed that could have given him a nasty bump. He was outraged. He went up to the ball and struck it as hard as he could off the fairway into some thick gorse.

At this the antagonism of the men behind us moved into quite a different gear. Two more balls sailed by quite close to us. Their conduct seemed now to be extremely dangerous. The McTeak was in no doubt that this was not the way to treat a clan leader. Traditional enmities might have been brushed under the carpet in these more enlightened and tourist-conscious times, but basic history is not so lightly dismissed. The caddie became very undignified and was matched by an extremely abrasive response. I looked pleadingly at Tiger, but I think both of us knew that the position was forlorn. The McTeak turned and walked towards them in what he hoped was a show of authority, but which seemed to the rest of us the action of an optimistic madman.

'I shall count to ten,' he said, 'and you will leave my course before I complete the count.'

If this was a forecast, I couldn't go along with it. The man in the tartan plus fours expressed surprise that The McTeak could count as far as ten. He put it more robustly than that, and The McTeak found his attitude inflammatory. Then the four of them burst past us, picking up The McTeak's ball as they went, dropped balls on the fairway and prepared to play in front of us. There is something particularly helpless about flouted authority when its bluff is called. The McTeak instructed the caddie to report back to the clubhouse at the double and call up reinforcements.

My own inclination was to let them get on with it. At least they were in front of us, and with The McTeak dictating our pace we should very soon lose contact with them; indeed our only concern would be that there wasn't similar trouble in the offing with the next party behind us. But this wasn't the clan leader's style. There was honour involved now.

[123]

Ten minutes later the secretary appeared with the caddie in a very flustered state. The McTeak told him briefly what had happened, and ordered him to have the fourball removed. The secretary was most put out to be given these instructions, which he obviously realised were not only impractical, given the nature of the customers involved, but might involve him in physical danger.

The McTeak waited for his response.

'I'll tell them they are being warned off for dangerous play and I shall call up the police to support me.'

The McTeak looked at him approvingly. 'We're behind you,' he said. That much I was glad of; I hoped it would be a long way behind.

We watched the secretary set off in pursuit of the unruly fourball. I shouldn't have wished to change places with him, but he marched up to them unflinchingly and delivered his message – that he was warning them off the course for dangerous play, and that their continued presence on club property would constitute a trespass, and that the police would intervene if there was any hint of trouble. Whether or not he had any vestige of the law on his side, I'm rather doubtful; but I had to give him full marks for pressing home his kamikaze mission. The fourball looked momentarily taken aback, but then started coming up with suggestions which the secretary found uncomfortable. He finally withdrew in as dignified a manner as he could, warning them that there was nothing for it now but the arrival of the police.

The visitors were not to know this but there was locally a manpower problem with the Force. The district, to its credit, was not a hotbed of crime, nor indeed a centre of much population since the McTeak Diaspora had stripped the locality of its traditional backbone. So it fell principally to PC Mackenzie and his motorcycle to enforce the rule of law in the field. Mackenzie was a conscientious, long-serving policeman, who relied on his uniformed presence rather than spur of the moment ingenuity. His delivery was slow, but he was undeflectable, and he was a good man for a holding operation if only because his handwriting was unusually slow. The secretary went back to the clubhouse and rang the police station number where he was relieved to find WPC Wendy Colenso available to take his call, having just popped in to catch up on some paperwork and get her mother some envelopes.

She listened gravely while the secretary broke news of the crisis. It was the president's presence at the club which was exacerbating the situation.

'I'll try and raise Jock,' said WPC Colenso.

'Good girl,' said the secretary, 'I'll hold on here.'

PC Mackenzie was having a quick game of darts in the Braw Lassie in Duncalkin when the alert sounded. He listened to the telephoned posting attentively.

'Sorry, lads,' he said, 'got to go.'

'Trouble?' asked the publican.

'A turmoil at the golf club,' PC Mackenzie explained and pulled on his gauntlets, went out to his motor bicycle, then came into the Braw Lassie again to collect his cap.

'Good luck, Jock,' said the publican, wiping round the rim of a glass and holding it up against what little light there was from the window of the tap room. 'See you this evening.'

'Ay,' said the constable, 'all being well.'

There was inevitably a hold up in the process of law, during which the malefactors continued on ahead while we began to incense yet another fourball behind us. The McTeak, in the confidence of his presidential position, made no concessions to reasonable behaviour. I watched the process with increasing interest. Personally I thought the malefactors had grounds for complaint, but I suspected that authority was going to triumph simply because it was authority.

The arrival of PC Mackenzie confirmed that view. He parked his machine carefully beside the professional's shed, pulled off his gauntlets, and greeted the secretary who came skipping down the clubhouse steps to join him. The professional, obviously anxious to remain in a non-combatant role, thought he'd better cover the flank in case of a further influx of holiday riff-raff.

'And you could keep an eye on my machine,' PC Mackenzie suggested. Then he set off with the secretary towards the malefactors, an unimpressive spearhead on the face of it but somehow hinting at reserves of strength. The process of law was on the march. The McTeak broke off to join it.

Tiger and I watched the confrontation. The malefactors were abusive but became progressively rattled. PC Mackenzie made enquiries of them and began to record their answers laboriously in his notebook. It smothered their fire.

They started, in their desperation, to appeal to his good nature. They expected he liked a round of golf himself; what would he say if there was a slowcoach straight out of the Ark in front? The McTeak bridled at the reference to himself in an Old Testament context and told the men that insolence would get them nowhere.

PC Mackenzie tipped back his cap:

'Don't wind me up, lads,' he warned, 'I'm just doing my job. It's nothing to me – it's just water over my head.'

By the time he had finished they were defused. We saw them trudge off towards the car park. The McTeak came back to join us, accompanied by PC Mackenzie and the secretary. He looked annoyed that we'd let the foursome behind us come through.

'Soon saw them off,' he said. There was something odious in his assumption of virtue.

Back in the clubhouse, the secretary confided in me. 'I didn't mention it to the president,' he said, 'but one of them was called McTeak.'

He must have been a victim of the diaspora, returning to his roots to show his pals the countryside of his ancestors. It was bequeathed almost entirely now to the custodianship of the clan chief. The rest of them had done well to go away.